A FIELD GUIDE TO
AMPHIBIANS and REPTILES
in ARIZONA

D0145686

Funding for this project was provided by the
Arizona Game and Fish Department Heritage Fund
and the Wallace Research Foundation.

April 2006
Arizona Game and Fish Department
2221 W. Greenway Road • Phoenix, AZ 85023

(602) 942–3000 • azgfd.gov

A FIELD GUIDE TO

AMPHIBIANS
and REPTILES
— *in Arizona* —

Thomas C. Brennan

Andrew T. Holycross

Arizona Game and Fish Department

2221 W. Greenway Road • Phoenix, AZ 85023

(602) 942–3000 • azgfd.gov

Acknowledgments

This publication is the result of a collaborative agreement between the Arizona Game and Fish Department and the School of Life Sciences at Arizona State University, a partnership fostered through Partners in Amphibian and Reptile Conservation. Additional funding provided by the Wallace Research Foundation.

We are especially grateful to Bruce Taubert, Kim Field, Roy Averill-Murray, Bob Miles, Heidi Hougham, and Valerie Boyarski for facilitating and promoting production of this book. Likewise, we are indebted to Randy Babb for sharing his extensive knowledge of Arizona's natural history and for his assistance with photography and artwork .

We thank the following people for guidance, assistance, and sharing their expertise: Roy Averill–Murray, Randy Babb, James Badman, Andy Baldwin, Bob Bezy, George Bradley, Moira Brennan, David E. Brown, Bill Burger, Geoff Carpenter, Jim Collins, Charles J. Cole, Betty Davidson, Dale DeNardo, Erik Enderson, Jerry Feldner, Kim Field, Darrel Frost, Bob Gaulden, Erik Gergus, Bob Hansen, Dave Hardy, Canyon Holycross, Dylan Holycross, Sharon Holycross, Craig Ivanyi, Tom Jones, Larry Kamees, Hans Koenig, Matthew Kwiatkowski, Jeffrey Lovich, Stephen Mackessy, Ernest Nigro, Erika Nowak, Charlie Painter, Trevor Persons, Bob Reed, Richard Retallick, Jim Rorabaugh, Phil Rosen, Cecil Schwalbe, Jeff Servoss, Wade Sherbrooke, Don Sias, Mike Sredl, Robert Stebbins, Larry Stevens, Brian Sullivan, Bruce Taubert, Marty Tuegel, and William Wells.

Line drawings by Randy Babb and T. C. Brennan.

Photograph credits and localities on pages 143–145.

About the cover: The Mexican Gartersnake (*Thamnophis eques*) is disappearing from much of its range in Arizona. Conservation and restoration of aquatic and riparian communities may help ensure the survival of remaining populations of this and other native aquatic amphibians and reptiles. Photograph taken by A. T. Holycross in Gila County.

Contents

Home to a richly varied terrain, Arizona is among the most biologically diverse states in the country. Elevations range from just 24 m (80') above mean sea level in the flat desert near Yuma to 3,854 m (12,643') at the summit of Humphrey's and Agassiz peaks near Flagstaff. A combination of diverse topography and location at the nexus of eight major biomes results in an extraordinary variety of often starkly contrasting biotic communities. All four North American deserts enter Arizona. The most diverse of these, the Sonoran Desert, is also the warmest and wettest. Although most associated with the iconic Saguaro and other cacti, the Sonoran Desert also encompasses vast expanses of low, shrubby desert, sand dunes, and other habitats. Mohave Desertscrub traverses the Colorado River in northwestern Arizona and brings its own endemic, the statuesque Joshua Tree. Fingers of Chihuahuan Desert extend into southeastern Arizona valleys, interdigitating with communities of Sonoran, Great Plains, and Sierra Madrean affinity, yielding an astounding diversity of amphibians and reptiles. Oak-rich Madrean Evergreen Woodland skirts the Sky Islands while coniferous forests cap their higher elevations. Across much of the lower Mogollon Rim, nearly impenetrable slopes of Interior Chaparral guard the transition from the deserts to woodlands. Great Basin Conifer Woodland marks the beginning of the snow tolerant communities found along and above the Mogollon Rim. The slopes of our larger mountain ranges and our high plateaus host some of the largest contiguous stands of Ponderosa Pine in the world. Across the relatively flat and cold Colorado Plateau sprawls Great Basin Desert, as well as expanses of Plains and Great Basin Grassland. The north slopes of a few lofty peaks shelter deep green Petran Subalpine Conifer Forest, filled with spruce and fir trees. There is even a small tract of treeless Alpine Tundra on the peaks of San Francisco Mountain, the highest point in the state. Several major riparian arteries weave through this landscape, from high in the pines down through the woodlands and deserts and ultimately to the Colorado River on the state's western border.

This conglomeration of communities harbors an equally remarkable assortment of 25 native amphibians and 107 native reptiles. Three introduced amphibians and six introduced reptiles have established reproducing populations in Arizona. Perhaps most surprising to the newcomer is the presence of 24 native frogs and toads from six different families. Representatives from Hylidae include the emerald green Arizona Treefrog (our state amphibian) and the Lowland Burrowing Treefrog, a frog of tropical origin that has adapted to life in the desert. Southern Arizona is home to the secretive cliff and cave dwelling Barking Frog (Leptodactylidae), as well as a tiny ant eater, the Great Plains Narrow-mouthed Toad (Microhylidae). An assortment of aquatic "true frogs" (Ranidae) dwell in the streams and ponds of our state; these include several species of native leopard frog and the extirpated Tarahumara Frog. Two introduced ranids, the American Bullfrog and Rio Grande Leopard Frog compete with and/or prey on native frogs, snakes, and other animals. Several "true toads"

(Bufonidae) can be found in Arizona, including the hefty Sonoran Desert Toad and the small, jewel-like Green Toad. Adept burrowers, spadefoots (Pelobatidae) emerge *en masse* after summer rains to breed and forage. Introduced to urban ponds in Tucson, the African Clawed Frog (Pipidae) does not appear to be expanding its range in Arizona. The Tiger Salamander (Ambystomatidae) is Arizona's only native salamander. Their life cycle includes aquatic larvae that can develop into cannibals, terrestrial adults, and individuals that reach adulthood in the larval form (neotenes).

Six turtles from three families are native to Arizona. The terrestrial and herbivorous Desert Tortoise (Testudinidae) reaches its highest densities on rocky slopes and bajadas within Arizona Upland Sonoran Desertscrub. The smaller, terrestrial Ornate Box Turtle (Emydidae) occupies the grassland valleys of southeastern Arizona. Three species of semi-aquatic mud turtle (Kinosternidae) dwell in permanent and temporary ponds, stock tanks, and streams across much of the southern half of Arizona. At least three species of non-native aquatic turtle have become established in the state.

Forty-nine species of lizard representing seven families are native to Arizona. Helodermatidae is the only family of dangerously venomous lizards in the world and is represented in Arizona by the iconic Gila Monster. Large and diverse, Iguanidae is represented in Arizona by 29 species and three subfamilies (Iguaninae, Phrynosomatinae, and Crotaphytinae). The omnivorous Desert Iguana that inhabits our hot, low deserts is in the same subfamily (Iguaninae) as the large Common Green Iguana of South America and Mexico. Phrynosomatinae includes animals as different as the speedy, thin, terrestrial Zebra-tailed Lizard, flat and squat horned lizards, and the Ornate Tree Lizard that is most often observed prowling in vertical environs. Fierce predators, several collared lizards and the Long-nosed Leopard Lizard (Crotaphytinae) prowl our deserts hunting insects and even other lizards. Ten native species of fleet-footed whiptail lizards (Teiidae) populate our low deserts and mountains. Our five secretive, colorful skinks (Scincidae) and the Madrean Alligator Lizard (Anguidae) tend to forage in leaf litter and dwell in moist areas in our woodlands and forests. Arizona's night lizards (Xantusiidae) are also secretive, although one appears to prefer rocky crevices, while the other is usually found beneath plant debris. Two species of gecko are found in the state. The Western Banded Gecko (Eublepharidae) occupies our deserts and the introduced Mediterranean House Gecko (Gekkonidae) is found on walls and buildings in urban environments.

Snake diversity is no less remarkable and includes 52 native species, 14 of which are dangerously venomous. More than one third of the world's rattlesnakes (13 species) are native to Arizona. One of our more famous serpents, the Sidewinder is specialized for life in sandy environs and inhabits low deserts and sand dunes. In contrast, the elegant and colorful Arizona Ridge-nosed Rattlesnake (our state reptile) lives high in oak and pine forests in just a few of our Sky Island mountain ranges. Like all Viperidae, rattlesnakes are highly venomous. Also venomous, the Sonoran Coralsnake belongs to Elapidae, a family that includes cobras, kraits, and seasnakes. Although Sonoran Coralsnakes have small mouths and rarely bite, their venom includes potent neurotoxins and they should not be handled. Our two small and worm-like threadsnakes (Leptotyphlopidae) are of primarily tropical origin and spend much of their time underground where they feed on ants and termites.

Although not nearly as large and powerful as some of its relatives, the Rosy Boa (Boidae) is an accomplished constrictor, sometimes squeezing a whole nest full of prey simultaneously. Most snakes in the state are harmless and are grouped together in the family Colubridae. Arizona representatives include several tiny "sand swimmers"; hook-nosed scorpion eaters; aquatic gartersnakes; large, swift, and diurnal whipsnakes; and snake-eating kingsnakes. A few colubrids, such as the Nightsnake, Western Lyresnake, Brown Vinesnake, and vibrantly colored Ring-necked Snake are mildly venomous, but harmless to humans.

Several of our amphibians and reptiles may not persist in Arizona much longer and some have already been extirpated. Experimental reintroduction programs are in place for some species, such as the Tarahumara Frog, but continued survival may be hampered by persisting threats. Unless the myriad factors threatening these species can be reduced or mitigated, Arizona risks losing many of its most unique species. Illegal collecting is probably a threat to the survival of isolated populations of a few species, but the greatest threats to amphibians and reptiles are generally more widespread and systemic. Introduced species, disease, the spread of agriculture, urban sprawl, water diversions, and heavy grazing have all resulted in substantial decreases in the geographic range and/or abundance of species or even entire biotic communities.

We hope that this book will foster a greater appreciation of Arizona's intriguing amphibians and reptiles and their fragile habitats. Prudent economic planning must include the preservation of intact ecosystems. Wild landscapes, complete with Gila Monsters, Desert Tortoises, and rattlesnakes are a significant draw in Arizona's tourism industry and contribute immeasurably to our quality of life. With responsible planning we can ensure that future generations of Arizona residents and visitors are able to enjoy the diversity of amphibians and reptiles that are an invaluable part of our natural heritage.

Andrew T. Holycross and Thomas C. Brennan
Tempe, Arizona
March 2006

Viewing Tips

Some of Arizona's amphibians and reptiles are quite conspicuous and can be easily observed by simply hiking in suitable habitat during appropriate weather. Most, however, require some degree of focused effort to locate. Many of our amphibians and some of our reptiles spend the majority of their lives underground, others are cryptic and difficult to spot even when in close proximity, and some are only found in remote areas that are difficult to access. By considering timing, environmental conditions, search methods, and habitat, you can greatly increase your chances of finding many of these animals.

Choosing the right time of the year and time of day is critical. Amphibians and reptiles are generally most active during the warmer months of the year (March–October). Many reptiles are active during the day in spring, when temperatures are relatively mild. In summer, when extremely high daytime temperatures deter diurnal surface activity, many animals become more active at twilight or during the night. Many of our frogs and toads don't surface until the summer monsoon rains, when they emerge to breed at temporary pools, often in large aggregations. To find these seemingly improbable desert denizens, drive deserted roads at night, a day or two after a rainstorm, and stop occasionally to listen for loud choruses of male toads. The cooler temperatures of fall allow many reptiles to return to surface activity during the day. Preferred ambient temperatures vary greatly among species, but recent rains dramatically increase your chances of seeing most amphibians and many reptiles.

"Road-riding" is one of the most popular and effective methods of finding amphibians and reptiles. This practice consists of driving slowly on remote paved roads that pass through suitable habitat. The twilight hours, just before and after sunset, are especially productive, although many species can be found late into the night. Scan the roadway and shoulder for animals crossing the road or soaking up heat from the pavement. To find nocturnal species that don't readily cross roads, try walking the desert at night with a large lantern, a practice far more enjoyable than sitting in a car. Road-riding and night walks are most effective for finding snakes, toads, and geckos. Most lizards are easiest to observe while hiking on mild days.

Many amphibians and reptiles are heard before they are seen. When in the field, listen for rustling in bushes or leaf litter, the rattling of disturbed gravel, or for the plaintive calls of male anurans. Take time to inspect shady retreats under bushes, the trunks of trees, and in crevices. A pocket mirror is handy for shining sunlight into dark recesses where animals often retreat during the day. Don't always expect to see movement, as many amphibians and reptiles remain motionless to avoid detection. Before entering an area take time to scan it with binoculars. Lizards can often be spotted basking atop distant rocks, though they often abandon these perches when approached. Thus, a good pair of binoculars is handy if one wishes to watch undisturbed lizard behavior. Likewise, scanning the opposite banks of ponds and streams allows one to spot and identify frogs or toads before they escape by leaping into the water.

Many species are closely associated with specific habitats and the probability of finding them increases considerably as one becomes familiar with their favored environs. When searching for a specific animal, consult the range maps, read through the habitat, microhabitat, and behavior information in this guide and tailor your search effort accordingly. The checklist in this book *(pp. 147–150)* will help you keep track of your observations.

Upon spotting an amphibian or reptile some may feel the instinct to immediately seize the specimen. Unfortunately, this practice results in missed opportunities to observe relatively undisturbed animal behavior in a natural setting. Watching and photographing animals that have not been disturbed by capture sometimes yields insights that help us more fully understand a species' natural history. This is especially true when one is fortunate enough to happen upon foraging or mating events.

Occasionally an observer may want to capture an animal to get a closer look or facilitate proper identification. A variety of methods may be employed to capture animals in the field. A fine mesh net with a long handle (dip net) aids in the capture of frogs, toads, and tadpoles. Many lizards are readily snared using a fishing pole with a small noose tied to the tip. A snake hook is handy for lifting and moving snakes and also works well for lifting debris or raking through leaf litter. Tongs are useful for extracting rattlesnakes from nooks and crannies. However, rattlesnakes are dangerous and should not be moved or captured by those who have not received proper training.

Please take great care to minimize habitat disturbance and destruction when searching for amphibians and reptiles. The places where these animals hide are their homes. If you must look under rocks, logs, or other objects, please carefully return them to their previous positions, so that they may continue to provide refuges for wildlife.

A fishing license issued by the Arizona Game and Fish Department allows you to capture or possess many of Arizona's amphibians and the introduced Spiny Softshell. A hunting license permits the capture and possession of most of our reptiles. Combination hunting/fishing licenses are also available. Current regulations prohibit spotlighting from a vehicle and use of prying devices to find and/or capture animals. Accounts that begin with the word **PROTECTED** indicate species that may not be handled, collected, or killed, even with a hunting or fishing license. Check with the Arizona Game and Fish Department for current bag and possession limits and changes to rules and regulations.

Most of Arizona is public land, and numerous State Parks, National Parks, National Forests, National Monuments, National Wildlife Refuges, and National Recreational Areas provide opportunities to find, observe, and photograph amphibians and reptiles. Tribal laws and regulations govern the collection of amphibians and reptiles on reservations. Public lands managed by the Bureau of Land Management, Arizona Game and Fish Department, National Forest Service, National Recreation Areas, and the Arizona State Land Department are open to hunting, including hunting for amphibians and reptiles. A hunting and/or fishing license is required for entry to most state land. Regulations regarding collection of amphibians and reptiles vary among land management agencies, so be sure to familiarize yourself with the rules before setting out.

Toad Toxins

Toads have skin glands that secrete toxins as a defense against predators. Most toads produce mildly poisonous toxins that only irritate predators' mouths. One of our toads, the Sonoran Desert Toad, produces highly potent toxins that can be dangerous or even fatal when ingested. Owners of cats and dogs should be alert to the potential for poisoning should their pet lick or bite a Sonoran Desert Toad. There is no antidote to toad toxin, so quick recognition of symptoms and help from a veterinarian can be critical. Toads pose little risk to humans who handle them, but people should wash their hands before touching their eyes, nose, and mouth.

Symptoms of poisoning (pets):
- Drooling and licking of lips.
- Pawing at mouth.
- Irregular heartbeat.
- Dazed or uncoordinated state.
- High body temperature.
- Seizures.
- Unconsciousness.

Treatment:
- If pet is conscious, rinse mouth with gentle flow of water from a hose. Do not force water into the throat. Rinse from the side of the mouth out the front.
- Flush eyes with water, if affected.
- Wet your pet's coat with water to help cool body temperature.
- Take your pet to a veterinarian immediately.

Snakebite

Snakebite. "How dangerous are they?" Rattlesnake and Gila Monster envenomations are rarely fatal when medically treated, but do pose a serious health risk. Rattlesnake envenomation usually results in intense pain and swelling and can include local tissue damage, loss of digits, and/or arthritis. Gila Monsters and Sonoran Coralsnakes bite only when handled. Gila Monster envenomation usually results in severe pain, swelling, and sometimes infection.

Avoidance. Most snakebite "victims" are envenomated due to their own carelessness or negligence. These incidents usually involve young men who have attempted to handle, move, provoke, or kill a rattlesnake. Left unmolested, most rattlesnakes will not attempt to strike people, which they perceive as possible predators. A rattlesnake's first line of defense is to take advantage of its cryptic coloration by remaining motionless and therefore unnoticed. Failing this, they often rattle and assume a defensive posture. Although defensive displays are intimidating and might seem aggressive, they are in fact purely defensive. Rattlesnakes sometimes crawl towards the safety of a hole or refuge when threatened, and if you are blocking their retreat, it might seem like they are "attacking." Rattlesnakes will strike to defend themselves, though this often requires substantial provocation. One often hears that a rattlesnake can strike a distance of half of its body length. However, because determining the length of a coiled snake is difficult, and because rattlesnakes are capable of moving quickly, it is best to stay ten feet or more away. **Do not push the limits.**

Another common question is, "What should I do if I hear a rattlesnake, but don't see it?" Stop, listen, look, and locate. Once you spot the snake, move cautiously in the opposite direction. Sudden movement might provoke a strike. Rattlesnakes sometimes congregate during the mating and denning seasons (late winter, spring, and fall). Move cautiously so that you don't step on a snake you haven't yet noticed and watch where you put your hands.

First Aid. In the event that you or a hiking partner are struck by a snake, a list of first aid "do's and don'ts" is provided below. While this is likely to be a traumatic experience, it is critical to remain calm and get to a hospital with emergency care facilities as soon as possible.

What to do:
- First, begin transporting the victim to the nearest medical facility for treatment and/or call for assistance, even if you are not sure if venom has been injected.
- Remove rings and other constrictive jewelry or clothing.
- Keep the victim calm and minimize physical activity to the extent possible.
- If possible, the victim should lie down, with the legs slightly elevated.

What NOT to do:
- NO ice or heat.
- NO electric shock.
- NO tourniquets or "pressure bandages".
- NO cutting, suction, or venom extraction devices.
- Do NOT attempt to kill or handle the rattlesnake.
- The victim should NOT drive, if at all avoidable. If no other transportation or phone is available, drive to the nearest help or phone and no further.

ARIZONA POISON CONTROL CENTER
1-800-222-1222

Methods

Natural and life history information (*e.g.,* diet, clutch sizes, mating season) is based on the scientific literature as well as reliable unpublished observations (ours and our colleagues).

Measures. All lengths provided for salamanders, frogs, and lizards in this guide are snout to vent length (SVL). In the amphibians, this is the distance from the tip of the snout to the opening of the vent, whereas in lizards it is measured from the tip of the snout to the posterior edge of the cloacal scute. The tail (if present) is not included in SVL measurements. Measurements for snakes are total length (tip of the snout to the tip of the tail, not including the rattle). Shell length is provided for turtles. Animal measurements are provided in millimeters (mm) and inches ("). Elevations are provided in meters (m) and feet (').

Common and scientific names used in this guide generally follow the recommendations of the Society for the Study of Amphibians and Reptiles, American Society of Ichthyologists and Herpetologists, and the Herpetologist's League (Crother *et al.* 2000. Herpetological Circular 29. Society for the Study of Amphibians and Reptiles. 82 pp.; Crother *et al.* 2003. Herpetological Review 34:196–203). We note the exceptions here. We use the common name "Arizona Treefrog" for *Hyla wrightorum*. We follow the recommendation of Douglas *et al.* (2002. Pp. 11–50 in Biology of the Vipers. Eagle Mountain Publishing, Eagle Mountain, Utah) with regard to the recognition of *Crotalus cerberus* (Arizona Black Rattlesnake). We recognize *Rana subaquavocalis* (Ramsey Canyon Leopard Frog) as conspecific with *Rana chiricahuensis* (Chiricahua Leopard Frog) based (in part) on evidence presented in Goldberg *et al.* (2004. Journal of Herpetology 38:313–319). We follow Faivovich *et al.* (2005. Bulletin of the American Museum of Natural History 294:1–240) with regard to placement of *Pternohyla* in the synonymy of *Smilisca,* and Crawford and Smith (2005. Molecular Phylogenetics and Evolution 35:536–555) with regard to elevation of subgenus *Craugastor* to genus rank. Taxonomic changes proposed by Frost *et al* (2006. The Amphibian Tree of Life. Bulletin of the American Museum of Natural History, No. 297. 370 pp.) and Mulcahy *et al.* (2006. Molecular Ecology 15:1807-1826) were published after this book was in press and will be considered for incorporation in future editions.

We use "Mohave" over "Mojave". Neither English nor Spanish, this word is of Native American origin. The U.S. Board on Geographic Names recognizes "Mohave" as the correct spelling for most so-named geographic features in Arizona, but lists "Mojave" as a variant (and vice versa, albeit less frequently). Both the Fort and County were originally spelled "Mohave" (Barnes. 1988. Arizona Place Names. University of Arizona Press, Tucson. 503 pp.).

Geographic Range Maps

The range maps represent our best estimates of where species can be expected in Arizona. The maps for the amphibians, lizards, and turtles are based on our observations, examination of miscellaneous museum records, information provided by colleagues, and our knowledge of species' habitat associations. The range maps for the snakes are based on an examination of all available museum specimens and our knowledge of species' habitat associations.

Areas where the species is expected to occur (in appropriate habitat).

Historic range from which the species appears to be extirpated. Isolated or very low density populations might still be present, but have not been reported for a decade or more.

Areas where the species has been introduced.

Arizona Map

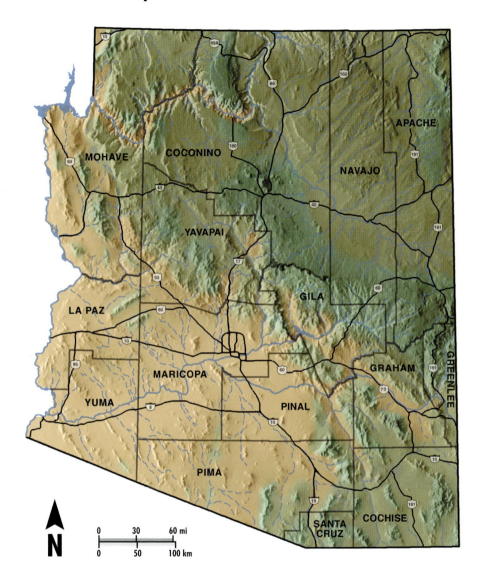

*B*iotic communities are characterized by distinctive groups of interdependent plants and animals. They are generally regional in scope and are shaped by climatic factors such as temperature and precipitation as well as soil characteristics such as nutrient levels and drainage.

Arizona's major biotic communities (mapped on the facing page) are intersected by numerous creeks and rivers that stretch from high in the mountains down through the woodlands and across the low deserts. Scores of specialized plants and animals make their homes in and along these streams and rivers. Referred to as "riparian", these biological communities contribute substantially to southwestern biodiversity and are critical components of complex southwestern ecosystems. Characterized by organisms with high water requirements such as tall broad-leaved trees, fish, and frogs, riparian corridors often starkly contrast with the surrounding biotic community. River corridors in low desertscrub communities are often lined with mesquite trees, Desert Willow, Seepwillow, reeds, Saltcedar, and cottonwoods. At middle elevations cottonwoods and willows become more prevalent and are joined by alder, ash, walnut, and sycamore trees. Arizona's highest elevation streams are lined by a variety of trees including maples, elders, alders, and willows.

Dams, groundwater pumping, and water diversions have dried long stretches of many southwestern rivers and introduced species have altered many remaining riparian communities by displacing native plants and animals. It has been estimated that less than 10% of Arizona's riparian communities remain in their natural form. Only through aggressive restoration and recovery efforts can we help conserve these elements of Arizona's natural heritage.

Names of biotic communities follow Brown (1994. Biotic Communities. Southwestern United States and Northwestern Mexico. University of Utah Press, Salt Lake City. 342 pp.).

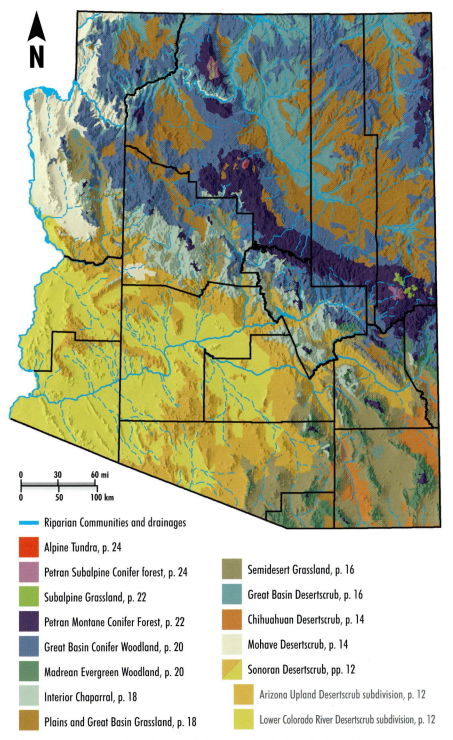

N

0 30 60 mi
0 50 100 km

Riparian Communities and drainages

Alpine Tundra, p. 24

Petran Subalpine Conifer forest, p. 24

Subalpine Grassland, p. 22

Petran Montane Conifer Forest, p. 22

Great Basin Conifer Woodland, p. 20

Madrean Evergreen Woodland, p. 20

Interior Chaparral, p. 18

Plains and Great Basin Grassland, p. 18

Semidesert Grassland, p. 16

Great Basin Desertscrub, p. 16

Chihuahuan Desertscrub, p. 14

Mohave Desertscrub, p. 14

Sonoran Desertscrub, pp. 12

Arizona Upland Desertscrub subdivision, p. 12

Lower Colorado River Desertscrub subdivision, p. 12

Adapted from: Brown, D. E. and C. H. Lowe. 1980. Biotic Communities of the Southwest. USDA Forest Service, General Technical Report RM-78. Color Map.

Sonoran Desertscrub: Lower Colorado River Desertscrub subdivision

Topography in this community generally consists of brushy flatlands transected by dry washes (24–400 m or 80–1,300'). This flat desert is found below the Arizona Upland Desertscrub subdivision of the Sonoran Desert. A combination of low annual rainfall (typically less than 200 mm or 8") and high temperatures make this Arizona's driest biotic community. Some regions regularly go a year or more without significant rainfall. Plants adapted to this xeric environment include Creosotebush, White Bursage, and Desert Saltbush. Washes are lined by trees such as Ironwood, Blue Paloverde, and Smoketree.

Amphibians and reptiles commonly encountered here include Couch's Spadefoot, Sonoran Desert Toad, Desert Iguana, Zebra-tailed Lizard, Desert Horned Lizard, Tiger Whiptail, Western Banded Gecko, Western Shovel-nosed Snake, Nightsnake, Gophersnake, Spotted Leaf-nosed Snake, Coachwhip, Long-nosed Snake, Sidewinder, and Mohave Rattlesnake. Less commonly encountered species associated with this community include the Sonoran Green Toad, Lowland Burrowing Treefrog, Yuman Desert Fringe-toed Lizard, Mohave Fringe-toed Lizard, Long-tailed Brush Lizard, and Flat-tailed Horned Lizard.

Sonoran Desertscrub: Arizona Upland Desertscrub subdivision

Typically found on low mountains, hills, and bajadas (300–1,050 m or 980–3,500'), this community is above the Lower Colorado River subdivision of the Sonoran Desert and below Interior Chaparral or Semidesert Grassland. Average annual rainfall ranges from 200–425 mm (8–17"), about 30–60% of which falls in summer. Saguaro, various cholla, various prickly-pear, Fishhook Pincushion, and Fishhook Barrel characterize this cactus-rich desert. The dominant trees are Foothill Paloverde, Blue Paloverde, Ironwood, Mesquite, and Cat-claw Acacia. Common shrubs include Brittlebush, Triangle-leaf Bursage, and Jojoba. Invasive non-native grasses now carpet much of this landscape and carry fire through a community that evolved in its absence. Consequently, large sections of this picturesque community are being converted to non-native grass and scrublands.

Amphibians and reptiles commonly encountered here include the Red-spotted Toad, Common Chuckwalla, Great Basin Collared Lizard, Sonoran Collared Lizard, Ornate Tree Lizard, Desert Spiny Lizard, Western Banded Gecko, Variable Sandsnake, Groundsnake, Nightsnake, Gophersnake, Western Patch-nosed Snake, Saddled Leaf-nosed Snake, Coachwhip, Common Kingsnake, Speckled Rattlesnake, and Western Diamond-backed Rattlesnake. Less commonly encountered species associated with this community include the Desert Tortoise, Red-backed Whiptail, Desert Night Lizard, Gila Monster, Western Threadsnake, Rosy Boa, Sonoran Coralsnake, Sonoran Shovel-nosed Snake, Western Lyresnake, and Tiger Rattlesnake.

Lower Colorado River Desertscrub in Rainbow Valley, Maricopa County, Arizona.

Arizona Upland Desertscrub in the McDowell Mountains, Maricopa County, Arizona.

Mohave Desertscrub

Topography in this community generally includes flatlands, plains, low hills, and bajadas (300–1,300 m or 980–4,270'). Mohave Desertscrub is often found below Great Basin Desertscrub, Great Basin Conifer Woodland, or Interior Chaparral and is sometimes adjacent to or mixed with Sonoran Desertscrub. Annual rainfall is low, averaging less than 200 mm (8") at most localities. Conspicuous shrubs in this xeric environment include Creosotebush, Desert Holly, White Burrobrush, Mohave Yucca, Blackbrush, and Shadscale. The Joshua Tree (pictured on facing page) is found only in Mohave Desertscrub.

Amphibians and reptiles commonly encountered here include the Red-spotted Toad, Desert Iguana, Common Chuckwalla, Great Basin Collared Lizard, Long-nosed Leopard Lizard, Zebra-tailed Lizard, Long-tailed Brush Lizard, Ornate Tree Lizard, Common Side-blotched Lizard, Desert Spiny Lizard, Desert Horned Lizard, Tiger Whiptail, Western Banded Gecko, Nightsnake, Gopher-snake, Coachwhip, Common Kingsnake, Long-nosed Snake, Sidewinder, Western Diamond-backed Rattlesnake, and Mohave Rattlesnake. Less commonly encountered species associated with this community include the Desert Tortoise, Desert Night Lizard, Gila Monster, Western Lyresnake, and Speckled Rattlesnake. Species found in riparian communities, springs, and other wetlands surrounded by Mohave Desertscrub include the Pacific Treefrog, Relict Leopard Frog and Lowland Leopard Frog.

Chihuahuan Desertscrub

In Arizona this community is generally found in flatlands and on hillsides and low sloping bajadas (900–1,200 m or 3,000–4,000'). It is often below Madrean Evergreen Woodland and adjacent to or mixed with Semidesert Grassland. Mean annual precipitation ranges from 200 mm to more than 300 mm (12"), more than half of which falls between May and September. A warm temperate desert characterized by hot summers and cold winters. Temperatures can reach freezing (or below) for more than 100 nights per year in some areas. Conspicuous plants include Creosotebush, Tarbush, Whitethorn Acacia, Ocotillo, Viscid Acacia, Allthorn, Mariola, and Texas Honey Mesquite.

Amphibians and reptiles commonly encountered here include Couch's Spadefoot, Mexican Spadefoot, Green Toad, Red-spotted Toad, Long-nosed Leopard Lizard, Common Lesser Earless Lizard, Ornate Tree Lizard, Desert Spiny Lizard, Regal Horned Lizard, Western Banded Gecko, Nightsnake, Gophersnake, Glossy Snake, Coachwhip, Common Kingsnake, Long-nosed Snake, Checkered Gartersnake, Western Diamond-backed Rattle-snake, and Mohave Rattlesnake. Less commonly encountered species associated with this community include the Greater Earless Lizard, Round-tailed Horned Lizard, New Mexico Threadsnake, and Chihuahuan Hook-nosed Snake. The Yellow Mud Turtle is found in or near aquatic habitats and riparian corridors within this community.

Mohave Desertscrub on Grapevine Mesa, Mohave County, Arizona.

Chihuahuan Desertscrub in San Simon Valley, Cochise County, Arizona.

Great Basin Desertscrub

Topography in this community generally consists of plateaus, low hills, and mesas (1,200–2,200 m or 3,940–7,200'). This desert community is often adjacent to or below Great Basin Conifer Woodland and Plains and Great Basin Grassland and sometimes above Mohave Desertscrub (e.g. in much of Grand Canyon). Low annual precipitation (averaging less than 250 mm or 10") is uniformly scattered throughout the year and much of it arrives as snow. Great Basin Desertscrub extends further north than any other North American desert. The presence of cold-temperate vegetation sets this desert apart from our other desert communities. Conspicuous plants include Big Sagebrush, Bigelow Sagebrush, Shadscale, Winterfat, and Blackbrush.

Commonly encountered amphibians and reptiles include the Great Basin Spadefoot, Mexican Spadefoot, Red-spotted Toad, Common Chuckwalla, Great Basin Collared Lizard, Eastern Collared Lizard, Long-nosed Leopard Lizard, Common Lesser Earless Lizard, Ornate Tree Lizard, Common Side-blotched Lizard, Plateau Lizard, Desert Spiny Lizard, Plateau Striped Whiptail, Tiger Whiptail, Nightsnake, Gophersnake, Glossy Snake, Striped Whipsnake, Western Rattlesnake, and Prairie Rattlesnake. Less commonly encountered species associated with this community include the Common Sagebrush Lizard and Pai Striped Whiptail.

Semidesert Grassland

In Arizona this community is most often found in low valleys and on rolling hills (1,100–1,700 m or 3,600–5,600'). Typically these grasslands are situated below Interior Chaparral or woodlands and are adjacent to or surrounded by desertscrub communities. Average annual rainfall ranges from 250–450 mm (10–18"), most of which falls during summer. Drought and overgrazing have contributed to substantial shrub invasion and desertification in much of Arizona's Semidesert Grassland. Consequently, many grassland communities in Arizona now resemble desertscrub. Winters are relatively mild with freezing temperatures occurring on less than 100–150 nights in an average year. Conspicuous plants include Tobosa, Hairy Grama, Palmilla, Sotol, Soaptree Yucca, and a variety of agave, cholla, and prickly-pear.

Amphibians and reptiles commonly encountered here include the Tiger Salamander, Couch's Spadefoot, Plains Spadefoot, Mexican Spadefoot, Green Toad, Woodhouse's Toad, Great Plains Toad, Eastern Collared Lizard, Elegant Earless Lizard, Common Lesser Earless Lizard, Southwestern Fence Lizard, Desert Grassland Whiptail, Gophersnake, Glossy Snake, Common Kingsnake, Long-nosed Snake, Checkered Gartersnake, Western Diamond-backed Rattlesnake, and Mohave Rattlesnake. Less commonly encountered species associated with this community include the Ornate Box Turtle, Texas Horned Lizard, Arizona Striped Whiptail, Great Plains Skink, Plains Black-headed Snake, Ring-necked Snake, Western Hog-nosed Snake, Chihuahuan Hook-nosed Snake, Milksnake, and Massasauga. In Arizona, the Plains Leopard Frog is found in riparian corridors, ponds, and other wetlands within this community.

Great Basin Desertscrub on the Kanab Plateau, Coconino County, Arizona.

Semidesert Grassland near Oracle Junction, Pinal County, Arizona.

17

Plains and Great Basin Grassland

Topography in this community generally consists of flat and open plains, but also includes low mesas and rolling hills (1,500–2,300 m or 5,000–7,550'). Usually below Great Basin Conifer Woodland and above Great Basin Desertscrub, in southeastern Arizona it adjoins Madrean Evergreen Woodland. Average annual rainfall ranges from 300–500 mm (12–20"), much of which comes from summer thunderstorms. This community has evolved with regular cycles of lightning-caused summer fires which were carried across large areas by wind. Fire suppression and cattle grazing have reduced the spread of natural fires in this community. These disruptions, along with extended droughts, have resulted in the invasion of weedy annuals, shrubs and Great Basin Conifer Woodland. Conspicuous plants now include Fourwing Saltbush, Snakeweed, Mormon Tea, and Soapweed Yucca. The grasses that used to dominate this community include Blue Grama, Galleta, Indian Ricegrass, and Alkalai Sacaton.

Amphibians and reptiles commonly encountered here include the Tiger Salamander, Plains Spadefoot, Great Basin Spadefoot, Mexican Spadefoot, Woodhouse's Toad, Great Plains Toad, Great Basin Collared Lizard, Eastern Collared Lizard, Common Lesser Earless Lizard, Ornate Tree Lizard, Common Sagebrush Lizard, Plateau Lizard, Plateau Striped Whiptail, Nightsnake, Gophersnake, Glossy Snake, Striped Whipsnake, Western Rattlesnake, and Prairie Rattlesnake. Less commonly encountered species associated with this community include Slevin's Bunchgrass Lizard, Pai Striped Whiptail, Many-lined Skink, and Milksnake. The Northern Leopard Frog is found in riparian corridors and other wetlands within this community.

Interior Chaparral

In Arizona, this community is found on mountain slopes below the Mogollon Rim (1,050–2,150 m or 3,450–7,000'). It is usually situated above Arizona Upland Desertscrub or Semidesert Grassland, and below Great Basin Conifer Woodland or Petran Montane Conifer Forest. Average annual rainfall ranges from 350–600 mm (14–24"), virtually none of which falls from April–June. Interior Chaparral intermittently receives snow at its higher elevations. Vegetation consists of dense, difficult to penetrate, stands of large evergreen shrubs such as Shrub Live Oak, Manzanita, Birchleaf Mountain Mahogany, Skunkbush Sumac, Desert Ceanothus, silktassels, Hollyleaf Buckthorn, Cliffrose, Arizona Rosewood, and Desert Olive.

Amphibians and reptiles commonly encountered here include the Tiger Salamander, Red-spotted Toad, Arizona Toad, Woodhouse's Toad, Canyon Treefrog, Eastern Collared Lizard, Greater Earless Lizard, Common Lesser Earless Lizard, Ornate Tree Lizard, Common Side-blotched Lizard, Greater Short-horned Lizard, Gila Spotted Whiptail, Madrean Alligator Lizard, Gophersnake, Striped Whipsnake, Black-necked Gartersnake, Black-tailed Rattlesnake, and Arizona Black Rattlesnake. Less commonly encountered species associated with this community include Gilbert's Skink, Bezy's Night Lizard, Desert Night Lizard, Rosy Boa, Ring-necked Snake, and Sonoran Mountain Kingsnake. Species found in riparian communities and other wetlands surrounded by Interior Chaparral include the Lowland Leopard Frog, Sonora Mud Turtle, and Narrow-headed Gartersnake.

Plains Grassland near Lyman Lake, Apache County, Arizona.

Interior Chaparral in the Mazatzal Mountains, Maricopa County, Arizona.

Madrean Evergreen Woodland

This biotic community most often develops on mountain slopes and hills, but sometimes extends into adjacent grassland valleys (1,300–2,200 m or 4,250–7,200'). This woodland usually occurs below Petran Montane Conifer Forest and above Semidesert Grassland or rarely, desertscrub communities. In Arizona, average annual rainfall ranges from 400–600 mm (16–24"). Mild winters and wet summers facilitate the growth of many oaks, including Emory Oak, Arizona White Oak, Gray Oak, and Mexican Blue Oak. Other conspicuous trees found in this woodland include Alligator-bark Juniper, Mexican Pinyon, and Madrone. Rainbow Cactus, Barrel Cactus, Schott's Yucca, Banana Yucca, Sotol, Palmer's Agave, and Parry's Agave are the most noticeable plants in the understory.

Amphibians and reptiles commonly encountered here include the Canyon Treefrog, Ornate Tree Lizard, Striped Plateau Lizard, Clark's Spiny Lizard, Yarrow's Spiny Lizard, Greater Short-horned Lizard, Chihuahuan Spotted Whiptail, Sonoran Spotted Whiptail, Madrean Alligator Lizard, Eastern Patch-nosed Snake, Sonoran Whipsnake, Sonoran Mountain Kingsnake, Black-necked Gartersnake, Black-tailed Rattlesnake, Rock Rattlesnake, and Arizona Black Rattlesnake. Less commonly encountered species associated with this community include the Barking Frog, Arizona Treefrog, Canyon Spotted Whiptail, Mountain Skink, Yaqui Black-headed Snake, Chihuahuan Black-headed Snake, Ring-necked Snake, Thornscrub Hook-nosed Snake, Brown Vinesnake, Green Ratsnake, and Ridge-nosed Rattlesnake. Species found in riparian communities and other wetlands surrounded by Madrean Evergreen Woodland include the Lowland Leopard Frog, Chiricahua Leopard Frog, Tarahumara Frog, and Sonora Mud Turtle.

Great Basin Conifer Woodland

Sometimes referred to simply as Pinyon-Juniper Woodland, this community generally occupies foothills and lower mountain slopes, but above the Mogollon Rim it is found on the plains and hills of the Colorado Plateau (1,200–2,300 m or 4,000–7,500'). Below the Mogollon Rim this community typically occurs adjacent to or above Interior Chaparral and below Petran Montane Conifer Forest. Above the Mogollon Rim it is usually adjacent to Plains and Great Basin Grassland or Great Basin Desertscrub. Average annual precipitation ranges from 250-500 mm (10–20"). This woodland is well-adapted to a cold climate and usually experiences freezing temperatures on over 150 nights per year. Consistently low temperatures exclude evergreen oaks and other warm-temperate vegetation. This relatively low diversity community is dominated by Pinyon and junipers, including Rocky Mountain Juniper, Utah Juniper, Single-leaf Pinyon, and Rocky Mountain Pinyon. The understory is comprised of grasses and shrubs such as Big Sage.

Amphibians and reptiles commonly encountered here include the Tiger Salamander, Arizona Toad, Canyon Treefrog, Eastern Collared Lizard, Common Sagebrush Lizard, Plateau Lizard, Clark's Spiny Lizard, Greater Short-horned Lizard, Gila Spotted Whiptail, Madrean Alligator Lizard, Striped Whipsnake, Sonoran Mountain Kingsnake, Black-necked Gartersnake, Black-tailed Rattlesnake, and Arizona Black Rattlesnake. Less commonly encountered species associated with this community include Gilbert's Skink and the Ring-necked Snake. Species found in riparian communities and other wetlands surrounded by Great Basin Conifer Woodland include the Chiricahua Leopard Frog and Narrow-headed Gartersnake.

Madrean Evergreen Woodland in the Pajarito Mountains, Santa Cruz County, Arizona.

Great Basin Conifer Woodland in Tonto Basin, Gila County, Arizona.

Petran Montane Conifer Forest

This community is found on the slopes and peaks of our higher mountains, as well as across some of our high plateaus (2,000–3,050 m or 6,500–10,000'). It generally occurs above Interior Chaparral or Great Basin Conifer Woodland and below Petran Subalpine Conifer Forest. These forests are among the driest in North America with average annual rainfall ranging from 460–760 mm (18–30"). This community is dominated by Ponderosa Pine, but also includes Arizona White Pine, Douglas Fir, Gambel Oak, and New Mexican Locust. Frequent low intensity fires once maintained open stands of mature forest characterized by large Ponderosa Pine with an open, grassy understory. Active fire suppression and removal of fine fuels by overgrazing has decreased the frequency and spread of these fires. These changes in natural fire cycles have substantially increased the density of woody vegetation (understory shrubs and young Ponderosa Pines). Consequently, fire no longer maintains these forests, but results in catastrophic conflagrations and conversion of forest to shrubby grasslands or Interior Chaparral.

Amphibians and reptiles commonly encountered here include the Tiger Salamander, Arizona Toad, Canyon Treefrog, Arizona Treefrog, Western Chorus Frog, Striped Plateau Lizard, Plateau Lizard, Yarrow's Spiny Lizard, Greater Short-horned Lizard, Many-lined Skink, Gilbert's Skink, Madrean Alligator Lizard, Sonoran Mountain Kingsnake, Terrestrial Gartersnake, Black-tailed Rattlesnake, and Arizona Black Rattlesnake. Less commonly encountered species associated with this community include Slevin's Bunchgrass Lizard, Western Skink, Twin-spotted Rattlesnake, Rock Rattlesnake, and Ridge-nosed Rattlesnake. Species found in riparian communities, springs, and other wetlands surrounded by Petran Montane Conifer Forest include the Northern Leopard Frog, Chiricahua Leopard Frog, and Narrow-headed Gartersnake.

Subalpine Grassland

In Arizona, this community is usually found in high elevation valleys or on high rolling hills (2,500–3,500 m or 8,200–11,480'). Subalpine Grassland is usually adjacent to or surrounded by Petran Subalpine Conifer Forest. Average annual precipitation ranges from 500–1,150 mm (20–45"), much of it falling as snow. From October to May, snowpack usually covers these grasslands and the growing season is less than 100 days. This community is dominated by bunchgrasses, such as Arizona Fescue, that are accompanied by forbs including wild daisies, dandelions, larkspurs, asters, and clovers. Soils are not conducive to tree growth.

Few amphibians or reptiles are regularly encountered in this high, cold community. Some of the species that can be found include the Tiger Salamander, Western Chorus Frog, Plateau Lizard, Greater Short-horned Lizard, and Terrestrial Gartersnake. Species found in riparian communities and other wetlands surrounded by Subalpine Grassland include the Northern Leopard Frog and Chiricahua Leopard Frog.

Petran Montane Conifer Forest on Mount Ord, Mazatzal Mountains, Maricopa County, Arizona.

Subalpine Grassland, White Mountains, Apache County, Arizona.

Petran Subalpine Conifer Forest

Restricted to the slopes of Arizona's tallest mountains (2,450–3,800 m or 8,000–12,500'), usually above Petran Montane Conifer Forest and below Alpine Tundra. This community is very cold and relatively wet, receiving 635–1,000 mm (25–39") of annual precipitation via summer monsoons and winter snows. The growing season is usually fewer than 75 days per year, during which nighttime frosts are not uncommon. Engelmann Spruce and Corkbark Fir dominate and are joined by Aspen and Douglas Fir at the lower elevations. Dry sunny slopes are populated by White Pine and Bristlecone Pine.

Few amphibians or reptiles are regularly encountered in this high, cold forest community. Some of the species that can be found include the Western Chorus Frog, Slevin's Bunchgrass Lizard, Striped Plateau Lizard, Plateau Lizard, Yarrow's Spiny Lizard, Greater Short-horned Lizard, Madrean Alligator Lizard, Sonoran Mountain Kingsnake, Terrestrial Gartersnake, and Twin-spotted Rattlesnake. The Northern Leopard Frog is found in riparian corridors, ponds, and other wetlands within this community.

Alpine Tundra

In Arizona, this community only occurs on the high peaks of San Francisco Mountain (3,500–3,862 m or 11,500–12,633') near Flagstaff. It occurs above Petran Subalpine Conifer Forest. The growing season here is very brief. Severely cold temperatures and the scarcity of liquid water prevent trees from growing. Dominant growth consists of low-growing shrubs, herbaceous plants, lichens, and mosses. Some examples are Golden Avens, Parry's Lousewort, Moonwort, Wild Candytuft, Orange Sneezeweed, Strawberry, and Alpine Speedwell. The small parcel of Alpine Tundra on San Francisco Mountain is home to the San Francisco Groundsel, a small yellow-flowered plant found nowhere else in the world. The lower elevations of Alpine Tundra are penetrated by elements of Petran Subalpine Conifer Forest, including Engelmann Spruce, Corkbark Fir, and Bristlecone Pine.

No reptiles or amphibians have been documented from this community in Arizona. However, the Greater Short-horned Lizard has been found in Alpine Tundra in neighboring New Mexico and a Gophersnake was observed near treeline on San Francisco Mountain.

Petran Subalpine Conifer Forest, White Mountains, Apache County, Arizona.

Alpine Tundra, San Francisco Mountain, Coconino County, Arizona.

*S*alamanders comprise the order Caudata. Although similar in general body shape to lizards, salamanders lack scales and claws. Their moist and generally smooth skin often contains glands that secrete mucus and poisons. Salamanders also lack external ear openings, which is true of only some lizards. Vertical grooves on the sides of the body (called costal grooves because of their position above the ribs) help water move over the body.

Salamander life history is variable. Many salamanders are terrestrial as adults but breed and lay their eggs in water. Similar in overall body shape to adults, aquatic larvae differ in that they have external gills or gill slits. Most salamanders breed and lay their eggs on land. These eggs develop directly into terrestrial young. A few salamanders do not lay eggs at all, but give birth to fully developed young.

The Tiger Salamander, Arizona's only native salamander, belongs to the family Ambystomatidae, also known as Mole Salamanders. This New World family of stocky, blunt-headed salamander is found across much of North America from Canada through northeastern Mexico.

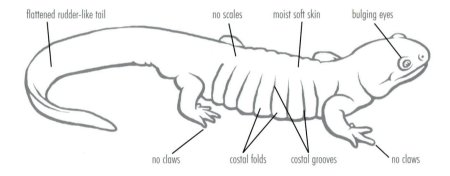

flattened rudder-like tail   no scales   moist soft skin   bulging eyes

no claws   costal folds   costal grooves   no claws

Tiger Salamander *Ambystoma tigrinum*

PROTECTED Arizona's only native salamander. Large and stocky (to 165 mm or 6.5") with a rounded snout, protruding eyes, and tubercles on the bottom of the front and hind feet. Terrestrial adults are generally olive-yellow with black spots or reticulations. Larvae are olive-gray with three protruding gills on each side of the neck. Some larvae become cannibals and develop a larger head and jaws. The rudder-like tail is flattened from side to side. Three forms occur in Arizona, the Barred, Sonoran, and Arizona Tiger Salamanders. Barred Tiger Salamanders are non-native and generally occur south of the Salt and Gila Rivers. Usually found from the grasslands up through Petran Montane Conifer Forest, but sometimes found as low as Arizona Upland Desertscrub. Adults are terrestrial, except neotenes (adults that retain their gills and overall larval form). Terrestrial adults spend much of their time in burrows or under surface objects near ponds, but can be found out crawling during humid or rainy weather. Larvae and neotenes occupy ponds, cattle tanks, lakes, streams, temporary pools and other water sources. Feeds on a variety of invertebrates and occasionally small vertebrates. Terrestrial adults return to the water to breed in winter, spring and occassionally summer. From 200 to 2,000 jelly-coated eggs are laid singly or in small clusters just below the surface of the water. Eggs take about three weeks to hatch. Because the larvae (referred to as waterdogs) are sold as bait, this salamander is often found in unusual places. Tiger Salamanders are carriers of chytrid fungus and iridovirus which can be lethal to other amphibians and they should never be transported between water sources. The Sonoran Tiger Salamander is listed as Endangered under the Endangered Species Act and may not be collected where it is found (in eastern Santa Cruz and southwestern Cochise counties).

Tiger Salamander
Ambystoma tigrinum

Barred
Tiger Salamander

tail flattened from
side to side

Sonoran Tiger Salamander

Arizona Tiger Salamander

gills

aquatic larva

*F*rogs and toads comprise the order Anura. Members of this order generally hatch from eggs as larvae (tadpoles) and undergo a metamorphosis in which their form and structure is radically reorganized into the tailless adult form.

Twenty-four native anurans, representing six families, can be found in Arizona (family names end in *-idae*). The toad-like frogs of Pelobatidae *(p. 32)* possess a spade-like tubercle on the underside of each rear foot. These aptly named Spadefoots have smooth skin, vertical pupils, and parotoid glands are absent or indiscernible. Most of our toads belong to Bufonidae *(pp. 34–37)*, characterized by conspicuous parotoid glands and warty skin. Many of the generally small and long-limbed frogs of the nearly cosmopolitan Hylidae *(p. 40 and Smilisca fodiens, p. 38)* are arboreal, hence the common name Treefrog. However, Treefrog is a bit of a misnomer for most Arizona species, which spend little time in trees. Members of Ranidae *(pp. 42–47)*, or True Frogs, have long, powerful hind limbs and webbed hind feet. Arizona's representatives from this cosmopolitan family include the aquatic leopard frogs, named for the spots on their backs. The Great Plains Narrow-mouthed Toad *(p. 38)* is Arizona's sole representative from the large and diverse Microhylidae. New World microhylids generally have smooth skin, stout bodies, and small, pointed heads. The primarily tropical Leptodactylidae is likewise represented in Arizona by a single species, the Barking Frog *(p. 38)*. This large and diverse New World family (as currently defined) probably does not represent a single evolutionary lineage of frogs. The introduced African Clawed Frog *(p. 46)* is in Pipidae.

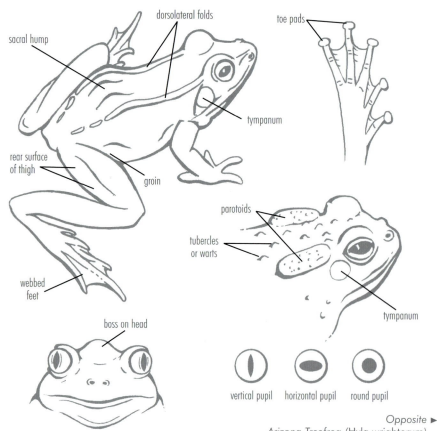

Opposite ▶
Arizona Treefrog (Hyla wrightorum)
Mogollon Plateau, Coconino County. Photo by T. C. Brennan

Couch's Spadefoot *Scaphiopus couchii*

A medium (to 89 mm or 3.5"), lime-green spadefoot. Females often have dark reticulations whereas males usually have faint markings or are plain. Lacks a boss on head *(see p. 30)*. Vertical pupils, dark sickle-shaped spades on hind feet, and lack of parotoids distinguish it from Sonoran Green Toad. Principally associated with desertscrub and grassland communities. Primarily nocturnal. Uses spades to burrow underground where it can remain for over a year during droughts. Eats invertebrates. Emerges during the monsoons to breed in rain pools. Call sounds like a bleating lamb. Eggs are laid in small masses and can hatch in less than 24 hours. Tadpoles can develop more rapidly than our other anurans (in as few as 8 days). Skin secretions may irritate nose and eyes.

Mexican Spadefoot *Spea multiplicata*

A small (to 64 mm or 2.5"), gray-brown spadefoot with dark blotches and red tubercles. Lacks a boss on head *(see p. 30)*. Eyes are copper with vertical pupils. Black wedge-shaped spades on hind feet and lack of parotoids distinguish it from Red-spotted Toad. Primarily a grassland species, but occupies communities ranging from Arizona Upland Desertscrub to Petran Montane Conifer Forest. Nocturnal. Uses its spades to burrow underground where it spends winter and dry months. Smells like peanut butter when handled. Eats insects, spiders, centipedes, and scorpions. The sound of thunder or vibrations from rainfall prompt emergence. Breeds and lays egg masses in rain pools during the monsoon. Call is a long, vibrating snore. Skin secretions may irritate nose and eyes.

Plains Spadefoot *Spea bombifrons*

A small (to 64 mm or 2.5"), reddish-brown to olive spadefoot with light stripes on the back, orange tubercles, vertical pupils, and a short upturned snout. Black wedge-shaped spades on hind feet. Two stripes form an hourglass shape on the back. Bony boss between the eyes and lack of peanut butter odor distinguish it from Mexican Spadefoot. The similar Great Basin Spadefoot has a glandular, rather than bony, boss. Found on grassland plains and valleys. Nocturnal. Uses its spades to burrow underground where it spends winter and dry months. Eats insects and spiders. Call is a series of rapid, raspy, often quack-like snores. Breeds and lays egg masses in rain pools in summer, and possibly spring in the north. Skin secretions may irritate nose and eyes.

Great Basin Spadefoot *Spea intermontana*

A small (to 64 mm or 2.5"), gray to olive spadefoot with light stripes and reddish tubercles on its back. Vertical pupils. Short, upturned snout. Wedge-shaped spades on hind feet. A boss between the eyes *(see p. 30)* distinguishes it from the similar Mexican Spadefoot and the Plains Spadefoot has a bony, rather than glandular, boss. Found from Great Basin Desertscrub to Petran Montane Conifer Forest. Uses its spades to burrow underground where it spends winter and dry months. When handled, it may smell like peanut butter. Eats insects and spiders. Call is a loud, grating *waa-waa*. Breeds and lays egg masses in pools in spring. Skin secretions may irritate nose and eyes.

dark, sickle-shaped spade on bottom of each hind foot

no parotoid glands

no boss between eyes

♂ Couch's Spadefoot
Scaphiopus couchii

♀ Couch's Spadefoot
Scaphiopus couchii

no boss between eyes

no parotoid glands

Mexican Spadefoot
Spea multiplicata

bony boss between eyes

no parotoid glands

stripes

Plains Spadefoot
Spea bombifrons

glandular boss between eyes

no parotoid glands

stripes

dark, wedge-shaped spade on bottom of each hind foot

Great Basin Spadefoot
Spea intermontana

Green Toad *Bufo debilis*

A small (to 50 mm or 2"), green to yellow-green toad with numerous irregularly shaped, small black spots on the back. The head is flat, pupils are horizontal, and parotoid glands are large and elongated. The spotted pattern of this toad distinguishes it from the superficially similar Sonoran Green Toad which has a reticulate pattern. Its flat head, horizontal pupils, and elongated parotoid glands distinguish it from Couch's Spadefoot. Found primarily in flatlands and valleys within Chihuahuan Desertscrub and Semidesert Grassland communities. A secretive burrower that spends most of its life underground or under surface cover. Usually observed only when it emerges to breed. Primarily nocturnal when active. Eats insects and other invertebrates. Breeds in temporary rain streams and pools from June through August. Call is a 3–7 second long, high-pitched, insect-like buzz. Usually calls from the cover of vegetation near the waters edge. Lays eggs singly or in small strings attached to underwater vegetation.

Sonoran Green Toad *Bufo retiformis*

A small, (to 64 mm or 2.5") yellow-green toad with a pattern of black reticulations covering the back and sides. A flat head, horizontal pupils, and large, sausage-shaped parotoid glands distinguish it from Couch's Spadefoot. Its reticulate pattern distinguishes it from the Green Toad, which has many small, irregularly shaped spots. Found in flats, valleys, and on gentle bajadas within Lower Colorado River Desertscrub, Semidesert Grassland, and Arizona Upland Desertscrub. This secretive toad remains hidden during daylight hours and emerges at nightfall during rainy periods. Eats insects and other invertebrates. The call is a 1–3 second long, high-pitched, wheezy buzz. Breeds in temporary pools, washes, cattle tanks, and ditches during the summer rainy season. Lays eggs singly or in clumps.

Red-spotted Toad *Bufo punctatus*

A small (to 76 mm or 3"), pale gray to tan toad with numerous small red tubercles and a flat head. Large adults sometimes lack red tubercles and may be a uniform gray or tan. Flat head, horizontal pupils, and small round parotoid glands distinguish it from the Mexican Spadefoot. This widespread toad is able to exist in some of the hottest and driest portions of the state as well as in some of our coldest forests. Found in communities ranging from Lower Colorado River Desertscrub to Petran Montane Conifer Forest. Usually encountered near temporary or permanent water along rocky creeks, washes, or in cattle tanks. In the extremely hot and dry portions of southwestern Arizona it is associated with springs and tinajas in rocky canyons. Abundant at the bottom of the Grand Canyon and in many of its tributaries. A nocturnal toad that seeks shelter in crevices or under rocks during the day. Eats insects and occasionally young toads. Breeds in spring and summer in creeks, rivers, temporary pools, and cattle tanks. Call is a long, clear, high-pitched, monotonous trill. Individual gelatinous eggs are laid on the bottom of pools or creeks. The eggs often drift together and blanket the bottom.

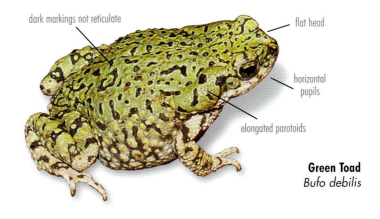

dark markings not reticulate

flat head

horizontal pupils

elongated parotoids

Green Toad
Bufo debilis

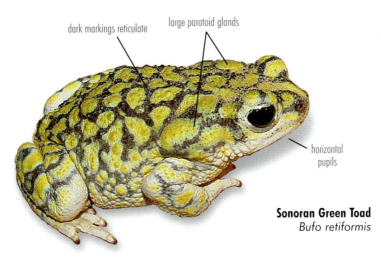

dark markings reticulate

large parotoid glands

horizontal pupils

Sonoran Green Toad
Bufo retiformis

round parotoid glands

Red-spotted Toad
Bufo punctatus

Arizona Toad *Bufo microscaphus*

A medium-sized (to 84 mm or 3.25") gray toad with a rusty, olive, or yellow hue and a light stripe between the eyes. The parotoid glands are large, oval shaped, and are often pale toward the front. Usually found along rocky, shallow streams from Arizona Upland Desertscrub to Petran Montane Conifer Forest. Alteration of habitat may be a threat to some populations. Hybridizes with Woodhouse's Toad where the two species overlap. Adults are nocturnal. Eats a variety of invertebrates, including insects. Breeds in streams in early spring independent of rainfall. The call is a musical trill, rising in pitch, ending abruptly after about 10 seconds. Eggs are laid in long strands.

Woodhouse's Toad *Bufo woodhousii*

A large (to 127 mm or 5"), bumpy toad with a prominent light mid-dorsal stripe. Olive to gray-brown with scattered dark spots on the back. Parotoid glands are sausage-shaped. Frequents areas with sandy soil near permanent and semi-permanent water in communities ranging from desertscrub up into woodland. Most abundant along river corridors and in farmland. Sometimes hybridizes with Red-spotted and Arizona toads. Eats insects and other invertebrates. The call is a 2–3 second long, nasal *w-a-a-a-h* that resembles the cry of an infant. Breeds in pools and sometimes in streams. Lays a clutch of over 10,000 eggs in long strands from February to September.

Great Plains Toad *Bufo cognatus*

A medium-sized (to 114 mm or 4.5"), gray, tan, or olive toad. Large, pale-bordered, dark blotches on the back are in symmetrical pairs, often separated by a faint mid-dorsal stripe. Occupies flatlands and low valleys in communities ranging from Lower Colorado River Desertscrub into grassland. A good burrower that spends most of its life underground. Eats ants, termites, other insects, spiders, and centipedes. Often found in large breeding congregations in temporary pools, ditches, and cattle tanks. The call is a long (to over 50 seconds), extremely loud, explosive, jackhammer-like trill. Breeds from spring through summer, predominantly during the monsoon. Eggs are laid in strands. Clutch size ranges from about 1,300 to over 45,000 eggs.

Sonoran Desert Toad *Bufo alvarius*

The largest toad in the United States (to 191 mm or 7.5"). Olive-green to brown with smooth, but lumpy skin. Young have small, orange-tipped tubercles. Its prominent parotoid glands distinguish it from the American Bullfrog. Generally a denizen of Sonoran and Chihuahuan desertscrub, but also found in Semidesert Grassland and Madrean Evergreen Woodland. Once known as the Colorado River Toad, it now appears to be extirpated from most of the Colorado River corridor. Eats invertebrates, lizards, small mammals, and amphibians. Call is a short (about 1 second), weak, rough, low-pitched *waugh*. Usually breeds in temporary pools formed by monsoon rains and lays its eggs in strands. Adults are often found far from water. Exudes toxic secretions that, if ingested, can cause hallucinations, paralysis, or death in dogs and other vertebrates.

oval parotoid glands

light stripe between eyes

usually lacks
dorsal stripe

Arizona Toad
Bufo microscaphus

sausage-shaped
parotoid glands

mid-dorsal
stripe

large paired blotches
with light borders

Great Plains Toad
Bufo cognatus

Woodhouse's Toad
Bufo woodhousii

Sonoran Desert Toad
Bufo alvarius

prominent parotoid glands

large white
tubercle

large glands
on hind limbs

Great Plains Narrow-mouthed Toad *Gastrophryne olivacea*

A tiny (to 41 mm or 1.6"), olive-brown or tan anuran with a stout body, smooth skin, and a pointed nose. A fold of skin crosses the back of the head. Small, dark blotches are usually present on the back, sides, and limbs. There is a tubercle on the underside of each hind foot. Found near flooded drainages, springs, cattle tanks, large puddles, and ponds from Lower Colorado River Desertscrub to Madrean Evergreen Woodland. A nocturnal amphibian that is most active after summer rains. During the day it hides in burrows, or under rocks, logs, or bark, near water. Feeds primarily on ants and termites. The call is a very short, high-pitched *peep* followed by a high-pitched, wheezy buzz that lasts 1–4 seconds. Breeds after summer rains and lays several hundred eggs in a thin film at the surface of the water. Skin secretions may irritate nose and eyes.

Barking Frog *Craugastor augusti*

A medium-sized (to 95 mm or 3.75"), olive-gray to rusty-gray frog with dark spots and a fold of skin across the back of the head. The head is wide and the hind legs are short and stocky. The skin is slightly granular and the toes are not webbed. Prominent, cleat-like tubercles are present on the underside of the feet below the joints. Juveniles are dark with a distinctive light band across the back. The fold of skin across the back of the head, a circular fold of skin forming a disc on the belly, and a lack of webbing on the feet distinguish this frog from the leopard frogs. A relic from Arizona's tropical past, this terrestrial frog has adapted to life in Madrean Evergreen Woodland in our Sky Island mountains. Usually observed at night near crevices on cliffs and large rock outcroppings, particularly limestone, rhyolite, and granite. Spends daylight hours in rock crevices, caves, mines, wells, or under rock piles. Eats invertebrates, including crickets, scorpions, centipedes, grasshoppers, spiders, and snails. Males call for only a few nights each year, usually immediately after the first monsoon rains. Call is a loud, distinctive, low-pitched *waaugh* that can be heard from nearly half a mile away. Large eggs are laid on land, usually in moist areas within or under rocks. An adult frog remains with the eggs and may excrete fluid to keep them moist. Young bypass the tadpole stage and hatch as fully formed frogs. Longevity can exceed seven years in the wild. A sighting of the species from the Sierra Ancha remains unconfirmed.

Lowland Burrowing Treefrog *Smilisca fodiens*

A small (to 64 mm or 2.5"), yellow-brown frog with large, reddish brown blotches outlined in cream or pale yellow. The snout is round, flattened, and bill-shaped, and a fold of skin runs along the back of the head. The skin atop the head is hard and firmly attached to the skull. Juveniles are green with a dark stripe between the eye and nare, and have a less prominent dorsal pattern. In Arizona, this frog is found near pools in mesquite-lined washes in Lower Colorado River Desertscrub and Semidesert Grassland. Primarily terrestrial, but adept at climbing and occasionally observed in the lower portions of mesquite trees. A remnant of Arizona's tropical thornscrub past, this frog has adapted to life in the desert. Spends the dry months and winter burrowed into moist clay soil. Uses its hard head to block the entrance to the burrow, and sheds many layers of skin to form a protective case around itself, which may help prevent desiccation. Emerges after the onset of the summer rainy season and congregates in temporary pools to breed. The call is a loud, raspy, metallic *wonk wonk wonk*. Eats insects and other invertebrates.

smooth skin

fold of skin

pointed snout

Great Plains Narrow-mouthed Toad
Gastrophryne olivacea

fold of skin

juvenile

adult

no webbing

Barking Frog
Craugastor augusti

juvenile

fold of skin

Lowland Burrowing Treefrog
Smilisca fodiens

adult

Canyon Treefrog *Hyla arenicolor*

A small (to 50 mm or 2") frog with rough skin and large rounded toe pads. Gray, tan, or olive with green or gray blotches. Can change color in response to environment. Often yellow on groin and inner thighs. Hind feet are webbed. Found from Arizona Upland Desertscrub through Petran Montane Conifer Forest. An excellent climber, it is usually observed on rocks, boulders, or cliffs near creeks, springs, or rivers. Sometimes found in rocky talus far from water. Eats insects, spiders, centipedes, and other invertebrates. Call is a series of low-pitched, metallic trills. Breeds in spring and summer. Lays eggs singly in streams and pools. Skin secretions will irritate nose and eyes.

Arizona Treefrog *Hyla wrightorum*

Our state amphibian. A small (to 57 mm or 2.25") bright green to copper frog with smooth skin, toe pads, and a dark eye stripe extending from the snout to the groin. The hind feet are mildly webbed. Eye stripe often breaks up into blotches posteriorly. The eye stripe of the similar looking Pacific Treefrog does not extend beyond the shoulder. Found in Madrean Evergreen Woodland and Petran Montane Conifer Forest, often in grassy areas after rains. Occasionally climbs into trees. Eats insects, spiders, earthworms, and other invertebrates. The call is a series of short, low-pitched *quacks*. Breeds during the summer rains in ponds, ciénegas, streams, and shallow flooded areas. Eggs are laid in masses attached to vegetation. Skin secretions may irritate nose and eyes.

Pacific Treefrog *Pseudacris regilla*

A small (to 50 mm or 2"), brown to green frog with toe pads and a dark eye stripe that extends from the snout to the shoulder. The hind feet are slightly webbed. The eye srtipe of the similar Arizona Treefrog extends beyond the shoulder. Found in grassy or reedy areas near permanent water. Native populations along the Colorado River occur in backwaters and marshes. Populations in the Virgin Mountains and in Phoenix and Tucson plant nurseries are introduced. Eats beetles, flies, ants, other insects, and spiders. The Pacific Treefrog's repeated *rib-bit* call is the frog call most often used in Hollywood movies. Breeds November–July. Egg masses are attached to underwater objects.

Western Chorus Frog *Pseudacris triseriata*

A tiny (to 40 mm or 1.5"), gray, brown, or olive frog with a dark eye stripe that extends from the snout to the groin. Usually has three additional stripes on the back distinguishing it from the Arizona Treefrog. Lacks toe pads. Hind feet are slightly webbed. Substances in the blood (cryoprotectants) protect cells and tissues from damage in freezing temperatures and help this terrestrial frog survive in cold Petran Montane Conifer and Petran Subalpine Conifer Forests. Found in moist meadows and grassy areas near ponds. Calls earlier than any other Arizona anuran, often while snow is still on the ground. Call is a high-pitched, vibrating *creeeak* that resembles the sound of running a finger over the teeth of a comb. Eats insects, spiders, and other invertebrates. Breeds November through August. Lays clusters of eggs on underwater vegetation.

Canyon Treefrog
Hyla arenicolor

bumpy skin

toe pads

Arizona Treefrog
Hyla wrightorum

smooth skin

eye stripe extends
beyond shoulder

toe pads

slightly rough skin

eye stripe ends
at shoulder

toe pads

Pacific Treefrog
Pseudacris regilla

stripes
on back

eye stripe extends
beyond shoulder

Western Chorus Frog
Pseudacris triseriata

Rio Grande Leopard Frog *Rana berlandieri*

NON-NATIVE A medium-sized (to 114 mm or 4.5"), green, tan, or olive-brown leopard frog with large dark spots. Dorsolateral folds are broken toward the rear of the body. Has large eyes and usually lacks spots on the snout. The hind feet are webbed. The rear surface of the thigh *(see p. 30)* is marked with dark reticulations on a light background. Light stripe on upper lip is usually faint or absent in front of eyes. Has larger eyes and is more likely to be green than the similar Lowland Leopard Frog. An invasive species native to Texas. In Arizona, it lives along river banks, canals, cattle tanks, and farmland ditches in Lower Colorado River Desertscrub. Introduced to the lower portions of the Colorado, Gila, Salt, and Agua Fria rivers where it likely competes with native frogs. It is expanding its range up the Salt River through Phoenix. Eats a wide variety of invertebrates and some small vertebrates. Call is a loud, rattling *brrrr brrrr*. Also makes short squawks that resemble the sound of a finger quickly stroking an inflated balloon. Breeds February to November. Egg masses are laid in shallow water and are attached to aquatic vegetation.

Plains Leopard Frog *Rana blairi*

PROTECTED A medium-sized (to 111 mm or 4.4"), light brown, tan, or olive leopard frog with dark spots. Dorsolateral folds are broken toward the rear of the body. A single dark spot usually adorns the snout. There is usually a light spot on the center of the tympanum and a light stripe along the entire upper lip. The rear surface of the thigh *(see p. 30)* is marked with dark reticulations on a light background. Lives in areas with temporary or permanent water such as cattle tanks, irrigation ditches, streams, and ponds within Semidesert Grassland and Madrean Evergreen Woodland. Appears to be extirpated from most of its historic range in Arizona; only two small populations remain. Eats a wide variety of invertebrates and some small vertebrate prey. The call is a series of 2–4 short, high-pitched, stuttering *chucks* followed by a low-pitched grunting or purring. Breeds from early April through early June and from August through October. Masses of up to several thousand eggs are laid in shallow water and are attached to aquatic vegetation.

Northern Leopard Frog *Rana pipiens*

PROTECTED A medium-sized (to 111 mm or 4.4"), green, brown, or yellow-green leopard frog with large light-bordered spots on the back. Specimens without spots are occasionally observed. A single dark spot usually adorns the snout and a light stripe may run along the entire upper lip. The only Arizona leopard frog with complete dorsolateral folds (not broken posteriorly). The rear surface of the thigh *(see p. 30)* is light colored with a few dark spots or blotches. Lives in permanent lakes, cattle tanks, creeks, ditches, and washes in Great Basin Desertscrub, Plains and Great Basin Grassland, Great Basin Conifer Woodland, and Petran Montane Conifer Forest. Sometimes forages far from water. The most cold tolerant of all leopard frogs, it hibernates in deep water below the ice. Eats a wide variety of invertebrates and some small vertebrate prey. Call is a long, low, rattling snore followed by chuckle and grunt calls. Breeds from March to June. Several thousand eggs are laid in a large, round mass. The Northern Leopard Frog is disappearing from much of its historic range in the United States, including Arizona.

posterior portion of dorsolateral fold broken

large eyes

usually no spots on snout

Rio Grande Leopard Frog
Rana berlandieri

pale spot in center of tympanum

spot on snout

posterior portion of dorsolateral fold broken

Plains Leopard Frog
Rana blairi

webbed hind feet

light borders around spots

Northern Leopard Frog
Rana pipiens

webbed hind feet

spot on snout

complete dorsolateral folds

light lip stripe

Relict Leopard Frog *Rana onca*

PROTECTED A medium-sized (to 89 mm or 3.5"), tan, gray-brown, or olive frog with scattered dark spots and dorsolateral folds that are indistinct posteriorly. Usually does not have a spot on snout. Light stripe on upper lip is usually faint or absent in front of the eye. The hind feet are webbed. The rear legs are shorter than those of the similar looking Lowland Leopard Frog. Found in streams, rivers, springs, ponds, and wetlands within Mohave Desertscrub. Eats invertebrates, and probably some small vertebrate prey. Males make a series of quiet, soft *cluck* calls during breeding season. Breeds primarily from January through April. Lays a mass of up to 250 eggs attached to vegetation just under the surface of the water, usually in February or March. Once thought to be extinct, this imperiled frog was rediscovered in 1991. It is now known to occur in just a few small populations. It is threatened by limited geographic range, alteration of aquatic habitat, low genetic variation, introduction of non-native plants and animals, and disease.

Lowland Leopard Frog *Rana yavapaiensis*

PROTECTED A medium (to 87 mm or 3.4"), tan or olive-brown frog with dark spots and dorsolateral folds that are broken posteriorly. Usually lacks spot(s) on snout. Light stripe on upper lip usually faint or absent in front of eye. Hind feet are webbed. Rear surface of thigh *(see p. 30)* is marked with dense dark reticulations. Has longer hind legs than the similar Relict Leopard Frog. Found from Sonoran Desertscrub to Great Basin Conifer Woodland and Madrean Evergreen Woodland. Lives in permanent or semi-permanent water. Usually found along streams or rivers with dense vegetation such as cottonwood and willow, but also in ponds, ciénegas, springs, cattle tanks, wetlands, and ditches. Introduced Rio Grande Leopard Frog may have displaced it in the lower Salt and Gila rivers. Eats invertebrates and some small vertebrate prey. Call is a low, grunting noise that resembles the sound of a finger stroking an inflated balloon, followed by a rapid series of 5–15 high-pitched, short chuckles. Breeds January through October and lays eggs in masses.

Chiricahua Leopard Frog *Rana chiricahuensis*

PROTECTED A medium to large (to 135 mm or 5.4"), stocky, green to brown frog with numerous small dark spots and relatively rough skin (for a leopard frog). Dorsolateral folds are broken toward the rear of the body. Usually green on the head and face. Light stripe on upper lip is usually faint or absent in front of eye. Eyes are higher on the head and more upturned than other Arizona leopard frogs. Hind feet are webbed. In adults, the rear surface of the thigh *(see p. 30)* is densely covered with light-tipped tubercles, usually on a dark background. Found in Semidesert Grassland, Madrean Evergreen Woodland, Great Basin Conifer Woodland, and Petran Montane Conifer Forest. This highly aquatic frog lives in grassy slow moving creeks and ciénegas, rocky pools within streams, permanent springs, beaver ponds, river side-channels, stock tanks, and ditches. Represented by two forms in Arizona: a northern (or Mogollon Rim) form and a southeastern form. These will likely be recognized as two different taxa in the future. Eats a wide variety of invertebrates and some small vertebrate prey. Call is made above or below the water's surface and consists of a 1–3 second long, low-pitched, hollow snore. Breeds February through September, usually commencing later in the northern population. Spherical egg masses are attached to underwater vegetation. Listed as Threatened under the Endangered Species Act.

dorsolateral fold
indistinct posteriorly

sporadic spotting

no spot(s)
on snout

Relict Leopard Frog
Rana onca

short hind legs

no spot(s)
on snout

dorsolateral
fold broken

**Lowland
Leopard Frog**
Rana yavapaiensis

many small
spots

Chiricahua Leopard Frog
Rana chiricahuensis

eyes upturned and
high on head

dorsolateral fold
broken

Mogollon Rim form

southeastern
Arizona form

45

Tarahumara Frog *Rana tarahumarae*

PROTECTED A medium-large (to 114 mm or 4.5"), brown, gray-green, or rust frog with rough skin and dark bars on the hind limbs. Dorsolateral folds are indistinct or lacking. No light stripe on upper lip. Tympanum is indistinct. The hind feet are webbed all the way to the tips of the toes. The similar looking American Bullfrog is larger, has smoother skin, a conspicuous tympanum, and a light colored chin. In Arizona, the Tarahumara Frog is found in permanent streams and creeks within Semidesert Grassland and Madrean Ever-  green Woodland where it is associated with deep plunge pools in rugged, rocky canyons. Eats insects, scorpions, centipedes, spiders, and some small vertebrates, including juvenile mud turtles, fish, and small snakes. Calls are made above and below the surface of the water and consist of soft, gentle snores and a variety of quiet grunts and peeps. Breeds and lays egg masses in the water April through May. This frog was extirpated from Arizona by the early 1980's. Tarahumara Frogs obtained in Mexico have been experimentally re-established in Santa Cruz County.

American Bullfrog *Rana catesbeiana*

NON-NATIVE The largest frog in Arizona (to 203 mm or 8"). Olive-green to brown with faint bands on the hind limbs of adults. The tympanum is large and the chin is pale. Face is usually green. Lacks oval-shaped spots and dorsolateral folds, distinguishing it from the leopard frogs. Lacks parotoids, distinguishing it from the Sonoran Desert Toad. Found in communities ranging from Lower Colorado River Desertscrub through Petran Montane Conifer Forest. Aquatic and dependent on permanent water for reproduction but capable of traveling several miles overland. Prefers deep and calm waters in rivers, lakes, streams,  ditches, and stock tanks. Eats almost anything it can swallow, including invertebrates, crayfish, fish, native frogs, bats, mammals, snakes (including rattlesnakes), and birds. Usually makes a *yip* call as it leaps into the water when frightened, unlike native leopard frogs. Call is loud, very low-pitched, and somewhat resembles a bellowing bull. Breeds spring to fall. Females lay clutches of up to 20,000 eggs in the water. Native to the eastern United States, this introduced frog is a threat to a host of native species including our native leopard frogs and the Mexican Gartersnake.

African Clawed Frog *Xenopus laevis*

NON-NATIVE A large (to 140 mm or 5.5"), olive to brown frog with a flat head, small front limbs, and large webbed hind feet. Small irregular spots or faint reticulations are sometimes present on the back. Small, round, lidless eyes are positioned atop the head. Pointed black claws extend from the three inside toes of each hind foot. No external tympanum. Introduced to urban ponds in Tucson. Occasionally reported in park ponds in  Phoenix. Highly aquatic, but able to move short distances overland during heavy rains and flooding. Eats invertebrates and small vertebrates, including native frogs and fishes. Calls are made underwater and consist of a series of short, two part trills. Breeds January through November. Several thousand eggs, laid individually or in small clusters, are deposited throughout the year. This frog was imported from Africa during the 1940s for use in human pregnancy testing. Escapees or released animals from this time period may have been the source of the lethal chytrid fungus that threatens native frogs.

indistinct dorsolateral folds

indistinct tympanum

rough skin

dark bars

webbed hind feet

Tarahumara Frog
Rana tarahumarae

no dorsolateral folds

white chin

large conspicuous tympanum

webbed hind feet

American Bullfrog
Rana catesbeiana

small lidless eyes on top of head

no tympanum

claws on hind feet

African Clawed Frog
Xenopus laevis

*T*urtles and tortoises comprise the order Testudines. Unique among the vertebrates, the bodies of these reptiles are encased by a bony shell that is fused with the spine, ribs, and pectoral girdle. Large plate-like scales or leathery skin covers the shell. The carapace (dorsal shell) and plastron (ventral shell) are fused together by a lateral bridge. All members of this order lay eggs, usually in excavated nests.

Six species from three families are native to Arizona. The diverse Emydidae is found on all continents except Australia and Antarctica. Most emydids, such as our native Painted Turtle and introduced Pond Slider *(p. 50)*, are semi-aquatic and associated with fresh water. A few, such as the Ornate Box Turtle *(p. 50)*, are terrestrial and superficially resemble tortoises (Testudinidae). True testudinids have a high, domed carapace and short, stocky limbs. This primarily herbivorous family includes the giant tortoises of the Galapagos Islands and is represented in Arizona by the Desert Tortoise *(p. 54 and opposite)*. Our three representatives of Kinosternidae *(p. 52)* are primarily carnivorous, semi-aquatic, and many release a foul-smelling musk when captured. Introduced Snapping Turtle *(p. 54)* and Spiny Softshell *(p. 54)* add Chelydridae and Trionychidae (respectively) to the list of turtle families found in Arizona.

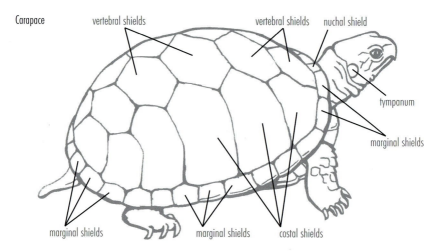

Carapace

vertebral shields   vertebral shields   nuchal shield

tympanum

marginal shields

marginal shields   marginal shields   costal shields

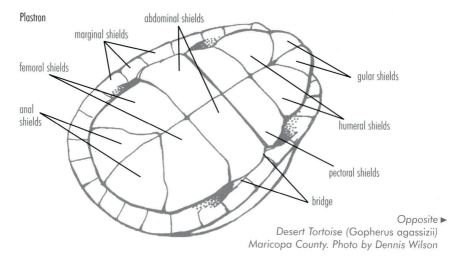

Plastron

abdominal shields

marginal shields

femoral shields

gular shields

anal shields

humeral shields

pectoral shields

bridge

Opposite ▶
Desert Tortoise (Gopherus agassizii)
Maricopa County. Photo by Dennis Wilson

Ornate Box Turtle *Terrapene ornata*

PROTECTED A small (to 146 mm or 5.75") land turtle with a dark, dome-shaped shell marked with radiating yellow lines. Shell becomes lighter and yellow lines become less distinct with age. Some older individuals are plain brownish yellow. The plastron is hinged so that it can be closed like a box when the turtle retreats into its shell. Mature males often have orange or red eyes, whereas females' eyes are yellow to orangish brown. Found primarily in flatlands and low valleys within Semidesert Grassland, Chihuahuan Desertscrub, and lower Madrean Evergreen Woodland. Infrequently found high in Sky Island mountain  ranges. Active during the day, particularly in the mornings. Activity is often stimulated by rain. Terrestrial, but adept at swimming and not infrequently observed in shallow puddles. Shelters in kangaroo rat burrows or in self-created burrows. May live to 30 years or more in the wild. Omnivorous. Feeds primarily on animals such as insects, worms, eggs, and carrion, but also eats cactus fruit, grasses, sprouts, and leaves. Breeding peaks in spring and fall. Females can retain eggs for several weeks until conditions are right for nesting. Buries 1–8 eggs in shallow nests within well drained soil.

Painted Turtle *Chrysemys picta*

A small to medium (to 250 mm or 10") aquatic turtle with a dark, smooth, low shell marked with yellow and red around the edges. The marginal shields are often marked with light lines and reticulations. The rear edge of the shell is smooth and the plastron is red to yellow with a single, large, dark patch in the center. Head and forelimbs are green to gray-green with prominent yellow to red striping. The similar Pond Slider differs in that it has 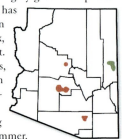 an orange-red patch on each side of the head. Native to the northern and eastern United States. Introduced to lakes and canals in Phoenix, Tucson, and Cottonwood. Populations in Apache County near St. Johns and Concho might be native. Normally inhabits ponds, lakes, and slow moving portions of rivers. Active during daylight and often seen basking on banks or on floating logs. Spends nights underwater on the bed of the pond, lake, or river. Eats insects, aquatic vertebrates, and plants. Breeds in spring and fall. Lays multiple 1–20 egg clutches in moist, shallow, underground nests in spring and early summer.

Pond Slider *Trachemys scripta*

NON-NATIVE A medium-sized (to 355 mm or 14") aquatic turtle with a low, mildly keeled shell marked with yellow and olive streaks. Shell often darkens with age and becomes uniformly colored. Rear edge of shell is serrated and the plastron is yellow with several large dark blotches. Head and limbs are green to brown with prominent yellow striping. A wide orange-red patch adorns each side of the head. The similar Painted Turtle lacks red patches on the head. Native to the eastern United States. Introduced to urban ponds and  canals in Phoenix, Tucson, and Yuma, as well as Montezuma Well, Wet Beaver Creek, and parts of the lower Gila and Salt rivers. Generally inhabits permanent, slow-moving water with abundant vegetation and a soft bed. Forages during the day and basks on rocks or floating logs well out from the shore. When frightened it quickly dives below the surface of the water. Spends nights on the bed of the lake or river. Eats invertebrates, aquatic vertebrates, and plants. Lays clutches of up to 25 eggs each in underground nests in spring and summer. Females grow to nearly twice the size of males.

yellow radiating lines

Ornate Box Turtle
Terrapene ornata

shell not keeled

no orange-red patch

rear edge of
shell smooth

Painted Turtle
Chrysemys picta

shell mildly keeled

orange-red patch

rear edge of
shell serrated

Pond Slider
Trachemys scripta

Arizona Mud Turtle *Kinosternon arizonense*

A small (to 152 mm or 6"), semi-aquatic turtle with a dome-shaped olive or brown shell that is flat or slightly concave on top. Marginal shields are often marked with yellow. The plastron is yellow and is hinged in front and back so it can close when the turtle retreats into its shell. There are fleshy projections under the chin and throat. The throat, chin, and sides of the face are plain yellow to cream, distinguishing it from the Sonora Mud Turtle. Similar in appearance to the Yellow Mud Turtle, but the first vertebral shield is not in contact with second marginal shield *(see p. 48).* Inhabits low valleys within Lower Colorado  River Desertscrub, Arizona Upland Desertscrub, and Semidesert Grassland. Frequents temporary water sources such as stock tanks, ponds, and roadside ditches. Spends most of the year in underground burrows avoiding dry and cold conditions. May remain underground for the entire season during a drought year. Most active during the day but occasionally observed at night. Often observed traveling overland during rainy periods. Eats toads, tadpoles, aquatic invertebrates, and insects. Breeds in summer and lays 2–7 eggs in underground nests. May emit an unpleasant odor when disturbed.

Yellow Mud Turtle *Kinosternon flavescens*

A small (to 165 mm or 6.5"), semi-aquatic turtle with a high olive-brown to yellow-brown shell that is flat or slightly concave on top. Marginal shields are often yellow. Plastron is yellow and hinged in front and back so it can close when the turtle retreats into its shell. There are fleshy projections under the chin and throat. Throat, chin, and sides of the face are plain yellow to cream, distinguishing it from the Sonora Mud Turtle. Similar in appearance to the Arizona Mud Turtle, but the first vertebral shield is in contact with second marginal shield *(see p. 48).* Occupies Chihuahuan Desertscrub and Semidesert Grassland.  Frequents ponds, puddles, and calm stretches of river. In Arizona it is usually found in permanent or temporary, shallow ponds and pools that have muddy or sandy bottoms. Most activity, including foraging, occurs during the day. Aestivates and hibernates in self-dug burrows on land avoiding the temperature extremes of summer and winter. Eats insects, snails, fish, frogs, and some plant material. Clutches of up to 10 eggs are laid in underground nests during the summer. Females may remain in the nest with the eggs for several days. May emit an unpleasant odor when disturbed.

Sonora Mud Turtle *Kinosternon sonoriense*

A small (to 175 mm or 7"), aquatic turtle with an olive-brown shell that has three, relatively indistinct, lengthwise keels. Plastron is yellow to brown and is hinged in front and back. There are fleshy projections under the chin and throat. Head and neck are olive-gray with distinct cream to yellow stripes and reticulations, distinguishing this species from our other mud turtles. The feet are webbed. Lives in rocky streams, creeks, rivers, cattle tanks, and ponds in communities ranging from Lower Colorado River Desertscrub to Petran Montane Conifer Forest. Also regularly found in ephemeral pools in rocky canyons and drainages. Often travels overland between bodies of water. Active during the day in spring and fall and at night during the hot summer months. Hibernates underwater or in cavities along the bank. Forages on the bottom of pools searching for insects, snails, fish, frogs, and some plants. Breeds in the water during spring and lays clutches of 1–11 eggs in underground nests. May emit an unpleasant odor when disturbed.

shell flat on top

Arizona Mud Turtle
Kinosternon arizonense

no reticulations

first vertebral shield
and second marginal
shield do not touch

shell flat on top

Yellow Mud Turtle
Kinosternon flavescens

no reticulations

first vertebral shield
touches second
marginal shield

ninth marginal
shield higher than eighth

shell keeled

Sonora Mud Turtle
Kinosternon sonoriense

projections
under chin

reticulations

eighth and ninth marginal shields
about the same height

Snapping Turtle *Chelydra serpentina*

NON-NATIVE A large (to 480 mm or 19"), heavy bodied, aquatic turtle with a powerful, sharp, hooked jaw and a long, spiked tail. The carapace is black to olive-brown and is often covered with algae or mud. The plastron is reduced, resulting in large limb openings. Native to the eastern United States. Introduced to urban lakes and canals in the Phoenix metropolitan area.

Normally inhabits the heavily vegetated, quiet waters of marshes, ponds, lakes, and rivers. Spends most of its time on the bottom of ponds or lakes, often partially concealed by plants, or buried in mud or plant debris. Rarely basks out of the water but may float near the sun-warmed surface. Overwinters beneath mud at the bottom of the lake or pond. Does not hesitate to bite. Its powerful jaws are capable of inflicting serious injury. Eats crayfish, fish, insects, snails, carrion, waterfowl, small mammals, and some plant material. Most breeding occurs in spring and summer. Lays from eight to over 100 eggs which are buried in nests on the bank.

Spiny Softshell *Apalone spinifera*

NON-NATIVE A large (to 470 mm or 18.5"), highly aquatic, pancake-shaped turtle. The carapace is smooth, leathery, and tan to olive with light margins. Young animals often have spots on the shell. The snout is pointed and snorkle-like. The feet are heavily webbed. Native to the eastern United States. Introduced to Arizona's desertscrub communi-

ties, where it has spread through the major slow-moving rivers, irrigation ditches, permanent lakes, urban lakes, and canals. Seems to prefer slow moving water with low banks of soft sand or mud. Rarely travels overland. Often basks by floating in warm surface water or by burying itself under the substrate in warm, shallow water where it uses its long neck to reach the surface to breath. Eats crayfish, worms, snails, insects, fish, amphibians, carrion, and plants. Breeds in April and May. Clutches of up to 39 eggs are laid in shallow underground nests during summer.

Desert Tortoise *Gopherus agassizii*

PROTECTED A large (to 381 mm or 15") tortoise with a gray to orange-brown dome-shaped shell marked with prominent growth lines. The plastron is tan to yellow and is not hinged. The hind limbs are stocky and elephant-like. Forelimbs are thick and covered with large, armor-like scales. When threatened, the head is pulled into the shell and the armored forelimbs are pulled back to cover the opening. Inhabits Arizona Upland Sonoran Desertscrub and Mohave Desertscrub. Sonoran Desert populations are found above the flats on rocky bajadas and hillsides. Mohave Desert populations are usually found in valleys with loamy soil or on bajadas. Shelters from the extreme heat of summer and the cold of winter in burrows it excavates below

rocks, boulders, or vegetation. Also uses naturally occurring rock shelters and cavities in wash banks. Most active in the relatively mild conditions of spring and during the summer monsoon rains. Eats grass, herbs, forbs, trees, shrubs, and succulents. Sonoran Desert populations breed in July and August and lay a single clutch of 3–12 eggs in a nest, usually within the burrow, the following June or July. Mohave Desert populations breed in spring and summer and lay 1–3 clutches of eggs April through July. Protected throughout its range in Arizona. Populations north and west of the Colorado River are listed as Threatened under the Endangered Species Act.

spiked tail

hooked jaw

Snapping Turtle
Chelydra serpentina

leathery shell

snorkel-like snout

webbed feet

Spiny Softshell
Apalone spinifera

distinct growth lines on shell

high domed carapace

thick, armored forelimbs

Desert Tortoise
Gopherus agassizii

*L*izards, together with snakes and amphisbaenians, comprise the order Squamata. However, the term 'lizard' includes many evolutionary lineages within Squamata, some of which are more closely related to snakes or amphisbaenians than they are to other lizards. Thus lizards (exclusive of snakes and amphisbaenians) do not comprise a natural evolutionary group. Nevertheless, we treat lizards and snakes separately in this field guide based on differences in natural history, public understanding of what constitutes a snake versus a lizard, and because entrenched common names usually include these terms. Although present in nearby Baja California (Mexico), amphisbaenians are absent from Arizona. Limblessness and limb reduction has evolved as many as 60 times in Squamata. Although the snakes and amphisbaenians take limblessness and related adaptations to the extreme, many other groups of lizards also have reduced limbs or have lost them altogether.

Seven families of lizard are native to Arizona. The largest and most diverse of these, Iguanidae, is represented in Arizona by three very different subfamilies, Crotaphytinae, Iguaninae, and Phrynosomatinae. A small and exclusively New World group, Crotaphytinae *(p. 60)* is represented in Arizona by four species. These aggressive predators have large heads with powerful jaws and run on their hind limbs in explosive bursts. Unlike most of our lizards they cannot regenerate their tails. Iguaninae *(p. 58)* species are primarily herbivorous, though some supplement their diet with prey. The large and diverse New World group Phrynosomatinae *(pp. 62–79)* is represented in Arizona by a wide variety of body shapes ranging from gracile tree-dwelling lizards to the flat and round horned lizards. Another New World group, Teiidae *(pp. 80–85)* or Whiptail Lizards, is characterized by long, thin bodies and tails, granular scales on the back, and active foraging behavior. Cylindrical bodies, reduced limbs, and hard, shiny scales characterize Scincidae *(pp. 86–89)*, a family found on every continent, save Antarctica. The Madrean Alligator Lizard *(p. 88)* is Arizona's sole representative of Anguidae, a family characterized by armor like scales and a soft fold of skin along each side that facilitates breathing. Unlike most geckos, eublepharids (Eublepharidae) such as our Western Banded Gecko *(p. 90)* have eyelids, lack toe pads, and are primarily terrestrial. Xantusiidae, or Night Lizards, are secretive, live-bearing, and have a soft fold of skin on their lower sides; two species *(p. 90)* occur in Arizona. Helodermatidae is the world's only family of dangerously venomous lizards. One species, the Gila Monster *(p. 92)*, inhabits Arizona. Although nearly cosmopolitan, Gekkonidae is only present in Arizona due to the introduction of the Mediterranean House Gecko *(p. 90)*.

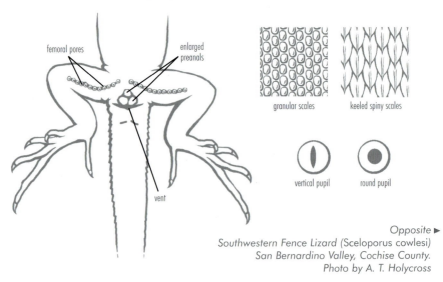

femoral pores

enlarged preanals

vent

granular scales

keeled spiny scales

vertical pupil

round pupil

Opposite ▶
Southwestern Fence Lizard (Sceloporus cowlesi)
San Bernardino Valley, Cochise County.
Photo by A. T. Holycross

Sonoran Spiny-tailed Iguana *Ctenosaura macrolopha*

NON-NATIVE A very large (to 310 mm or 12.25") ash gray to gray-brown lizard with black mottling and a long spiny tail. Dark bars cross the back and the posterior half of the tail is banded. Color may rapidly change from pale ash gray to dark gray. A row of enlarged mid-dorsal scales forms a low crest on the neck and a ridge down the back. Juveniles are bright green. Introduced to the grounds of the Arizona-Sonora Desert Museum (ASDM) near Tucson in the 1970s. It is still reproducing there, but apparently is not expanding its range, and is only occasionally observed off the Museum grounds. Diurnal. Frequently seen basking on rock outcrops, boulders, cacti, and trees in its native Mexico. Has also been observed on walls and fences in areas of human habitation. When threatened it retreats into rock crevices or woodpecker holes and uses its spiny tail to block out predators. Juveniles are predominantly arboreal. Herbivorous, but occasionally eats invertebrates and has been documented eating rodents and Clark's Spiny Lizards at ASDM. Lays eggs from spring through early summer.

Desert Iguana *Dipsosaurus dorsalis*

A large (to 146 mm or 5.75") lizard with a long tail, stocky limbs, and a small, blunt head. The back is usually gray to brown with white dots surrounded by reddish brown reticulations. The lower sides are cream or tan with reddish brown dots or dashes. Adults have a rust colored patch on each side of the belly during breeding season. Red-brown spots merge together to form bands on the tail. The tail is taller than it is wide. A row of enlarged, pointed scales runs down the midline of the back. Found in Mohave and Lower Colorado River desertscrub and sometimes in Arizona Upland Desertscrub. Frequents flatlands with sandy or clay soils, dunes, and gentle sloping bajadas. Active on very hot days, even when most other lizards are under cover. A ground dweller that will occasionally climb bushes to reach leaves and flowers, particularly the small yellow flowers of the Creosotebush. A very fast runner that often seeks refuge in burrows when frightened. Primarily herbivorous, but also eats insects and occasionally carrion. Breeds April to July and lays a clutch of up to 8 eggs in late spring or summer.

Common Chuckwalla *Sauromalus ater*

A large (to 229 mm or 9"), flat, wide, and heavy lizard with loose, baggy skin on the sides of the body and neck. Males have black heads and limbs and yellowish to light gray tails. In the south-central portion of the state males have black torsos. Males from Glen Canyon have pale ash gray torsos. Males in the remainder of the state have red torsos. Males on South Mountain (Maricopa County) have black torsos and bright orange tails. Females statewide are gray-brown with faint mottling or crossbars. Young are banded. Pattern and absence of large bead-like scales distinguish the Chuckwalla from the Gila Monster. Inhabits Sonoran, Mohave, and Great Basin desertscrub. A crevice dweller found in rocky habitats such as boulder piles, mountainsides, and lava fields. Often seen basking during the day. When threatened it usually retreats into a narrow crevice and inflates with air until securely wedged. Primarily herbivorous, but occasionally eats insects. Breeds May through June. Lays a clutch of up to 16 eggs in an underground nest in summer.

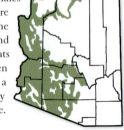

Sonoran Spiny-tailed Iguana
Ctenosaura macrolopha

ridge of enlarged scales

spiny scales
encircle tail

tail taller than it is wide

row of enlarged scales

small blunt
head

Desert Iguana
Dipsosaurus dorsalis

Common Chuckwalla
Sauromalus ater

loose folds of skin

Juvenile

Great Basin Collared Lizard *Crotaphytus bicinctores*

A medium-sized (to 108 mm or 4.25"), robust lizard with a large head and two black collars on the neck. Anterior collar encircles the throat on males. Gray-brown with light dots, yellow-orange suffusion on limbs, and soft-edged, yellow-orange crossbands. Tail taller than it is wide with a pale stripe down the top. Dark patches on throat and groin on males. Females lack tail stripe, are duller in color, and have orange bars on their sides when gravid. Inhabits rocky hillsides and canyons in Arizona's western and northern desertscrub communities. Often seen basking atop large rocks. Uses its powerful jaws to capture insects, spiders, and lizards. Occasionally eats plants. Lays 3–7 eggs in spring or summer. Hybridizes with *Crotaphytus collaris* (below) along contact zones.

Eastern Collared Lizard *Crotaphytus collaris*

A medium (to 108 mm or 4.25"), robust lizard with a large head and two black collars on the neck. Anterior collar does not encircle the throat. Gray to blue-green with yellow on head and front feet. Body has light spots and soft-edged, yellow crossbands. Tail is round in cross-section. Females are duller in color and have orange bars on their sides when gravid. Found from Arizona Upland Desertscrub through Great Basin Conifer Woodland. Often seen basking atop large rocks. Like other *Crotaphytus* this lizard is territorial, aggressive, and bites hard when captured. Uses powerful jaws to capture lizards, insects, and spiders. Occasionally eats plants. Lays 1–14 eggs in spring or summer. Hybridizes with *Crotaphytus bicinctores* (above) along contact zones.

Sonoran Collared Lizard *Crotaphytus nebrius*

A medium (to 108 mm or 4.25"), robust lizard with a large head and two black collar markings on the neck. Anterior collar encircles the throat on males. Brown to yellow-brown with large light spots on the back that become smaller on the sides. Some individuals lack spots. Tail is round in cross-section. Males have orange-brown coloration on the lower sides of the body during breeding season. Females are duller in color and have orange bars on their sides when gravid. Found on rocky bajadas, hills, and mountains in Sonoran Desertscrub. Often seen basking in the mid-morning sun atop large rocks and boulders. Eats invertebrates and small lizards. Lays eggs in spring or summer.

Long-nosed Leopard Lizard *Gambelia wislizenii*

A large (to 140 mm or 5.5") lizard with a long, rounded tail and a large, elongated head. Color can change from yellow-tan with dark spots to gray-brown with thin, pale, lace-like lines across the back and tail. Females have bright reddish orange markings on the head, neck, sides of body, and underside of tail during breeding season. Inhabits Arizona's desertscrub communities and Semidesert Grassland. Frequents open, brushy plains, low valleys, and gentle slopes. May squeak, hiss, or attempt to bite when captured. Its powerful jaws are capable of delivering a painful bite. An aggressive predator that eats invertebrates, lizards, snakes, and small mammals. Also eats some plant material. Breeds in spring and lays a clutch of up to 11 eggs in spring or summer.

pale stripe
on top of tail

**Great Basin
Collared Lizard**
Crotaphytus bicinctores

tail taller
than it is wide

faint
crossbars

**Eastern
Collared Lizard**
Crotaphytus collaris

rounded tail with
no stripe

rounded tail
with no stripe

collar often
broken dorsally

**Sonoran
Collared Lizard**
Crotaphytus nebrius

smaller light
spots on sides

spots and/or light lines

long round tail

**Long-nosed
Leopard Lizard**
Gambelia wislizenii

Zebra-tailed Lizard *Callisaurus draconoides*

A medium-sized (to 102 mm or 4") lizard with a flattened tail and long thin limbs. Dark tail bands become black ventrally, where they starkly contrast the white background. Body is yellow-tan with two dark side bars extending up from the belly just behind the forelimbs. On males, the side bars extend onto the belly where they are surrounded by blue patches. On females the bars are faint or absent and the belly lacks blue patches. 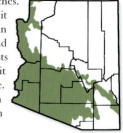 External ear openings and forward position of side bars distinguish it from the similar Greater Earless Lizard. A ground dweller found in flatlands and broad, sandy washes within Sonoran, Mohave, and Chihuahuan desertscrub. Flees from predators with explosive bursts of speed, running with its tail curled over its back. Between bursts, it often curls and wags its tail exposing the "zebra-striped" underside. Almost exclusively diurnal, but sometimes encountered asleep on the surface at night. Eats insects, spiders, and small lizards. Mates in spring. One or more clutches of 1–15 eggs are laid in summer.

Greater Earless Lizard *Cophosaurus texanus*

A medium-sized (to 89 mm or 3.5"), gray to tan lizard with a flattened tail and long thin limbs. Tail bands are faint dorsally, but become black ventrally, where they starkly contrast with the white background. Markings consist of brown, peach, orange, or salmon spots on the back that often fade into a wash of yellow above the hind limbs. Forelimbs are often tinted yellow. Two dark, crescent-shaped side bars extend up from the belly just in front of the hind limbs. Side bars are subdued or absent on females. On males, the side bars are surrounded by yellow dorsally and turquoise-blue ventrally. Females develop a salmon tint on the flanks and a pink throat patch during breeding season. Posterior position of side bars and lack of external ear openings distinguish it from the similar Zebra-tailed Lizard. An alert, fast-running ground dweller that is usually found above the flats on bajadas, hillsides, and mountain slopes in Arizona Upland Desertscrub, Semidesert Grassland, Interior Chaparral, and Great Basin Conifer Woodland. Seems to prefer sandy washes and relatively open, gravelly areas. Before fleeing, this lizard occasionally tail-wags and often runs with its tail curled over its back, exposing the prominent black on white underside. Almost exclusively diurnal. Eats grasshoppers, spiders, flying insects, beetles, and other invertebrates. Mates and lays clutches of 2–9 eggs in spring and summer.

ear opening

bars near front legs

Zebra-tailed Lizard
Callisaurus draconoides

no ear openings

bars near hind legs

Greater Earless Lizard
Cophosaurus texanus

Common Lesser Earless Lizard *Holbrookia maculata*

A small (to 70 mm or 2.75"), gray to orange-brown lizard with a short tail and no external ear openings. Coloration often closely matches the soil on which the lizard lives. Markings are quite variable, but usually include light spots or speckles and four rows of blotches or chevrons on the body. Some specimens lack markings. There are usually paired blotches on the lower sides of the body. Males often have blue coloration around bold side blotches, less distinct dorsal blotches, light speckling, and yellow on the lower sides. Females have a pink or orange tint when gravid, and side blotches are often faint or lacking. Underside of tail is plain white, distinguishing it from the Zebra-tailed and Greater Earless Lizard. Twin side bars and lack of ear openings distinguish it from Common Side-blotched Lizard. The similar Elegant Earless Lizard is larger, usually has a longer tail (longer than snout-vent length), and has longer hind limbs and feet (toe reaches eye when hind leg carried forward). Found in communities ranging from Semidesert Grassland up into woodland. Often seen in relatively flat, open, and sparsely vegetated areas with sandy or gravelly soil. Faded edges on range map indicate an ill-defined species boundary with the Elegant Earless Lizard. A diurnal ground dweller that is most active in mornings and evenings during the hotter months. Active all day during spring and early fall. Sometimes encountered on paved roads at night. Eats insects, spiders, and hatchling lizards. Mates in spring. Lays one or two clutches of 1–10 eggs each in spring and summer.

Elegant Earless Lizard *Holbrookia elegans*

A small (to 75 mm or 3"), gray to orange-brown lizard with no external ear openings. Coloration often closely matches the soil on which the lizard lives. Markings are highly variable, but usually include four rows of blotches or chevrons on the body and light speckles. Some individuals lack markings. There are usually paired blotches on the sides of the body. Males often have blue coloration around bold side blotches, less distinct dorsal blotches, light speckling, and yellow infusion on the lower sides. Females have a pink or orange tint when gravid, and side blotches are often faint or lacking. Underside of tail is plain white, distinguishing it from the Zebra-tailed and Greater Earless Lizard. Twin side bars and lack of ear openings distinguish it from Common Side-blotched Lizard. The similar Common Lesser Earless Lizard is smaller, usually has a shorter tail (usually shorter than snout-vent length), and shorter hind limbs and feet (toe usually does not reach eye when hind leg carried forward). Found in Semidesert Grassland, Chihuahuan Desertscrub, Arizona Upland Desertscrub, and Madrean Evergreen Woodland. Usually observed in relatively open, sparsely vegetated areas with sandy or gravelly soil. Faded edges on range map indicate an ill-defined species boundary with the Common Lesser Earless Lizard. This diurnal ground dweller is most active in mornings and evenings, avoiding the extreme mid-day heat. Occasionally nocturnal. Eats insects, spiders, and hatchling lizards. Mates in spring. Lays one or two clutches of eggs in spring and summer.

no ear
opening

♂

short tail

two blotches
near front legs

no banding
on tail

♂

Common Lesser Earless Lizard
Holbrookia maculata

no ear
opening

♀

long tail

two blotches
near front legs

♂

Elegant Earless Lizard
Holbrookia elegans

Yuman Desert Fringe-toed Lizard *Uma rufopunctata*

A medium-sized (to 120 mm or 4.75"), pale cream, tan, to reddish brown, sand-dwelling lizard with a flat body, a flattened tail, and a chisel-like snout. The edges of the toes on the hind feet are fringed with enlarged and pointed scales that expand surface area and therefore increase traction on fine sand. Coloration usually closely matches the sand, helping the lizard avoid detection by predators. Additional adaptations for living on and burrowing in sand include a chisel-shaped head, countersunk lower jaw, overlapping and interlocking eyelids, flaps over the ear openings, and valves in the nostrils. Markings consist of small orange dots surrounded by black reticulations that merge into lines on the anterior portion of the back. The underside is white with a black spot on each side of the belly and black bars under the tail. The lines in the back pattern, orange bars on the sides of the belly during breeding season, and lines on throat distinguish it from the similar Mohave Fringe-toed Lizard. Found on and around dunes and sandy flats with sparse vegetation in Lower Colorado River Desertscrub. This speedy, diurnal ground dweller often runs on its hind feet when fleeing. After running a short distance it often wriggles head first into loose sand, thereby rapidly burying itself. Burrows of other animals are also used as refuges. Eats insects, small lizards, and some plant material. Mates in spring. Lays clutches of 1–5 eggs in spring and summer. Eggs are laid in underground nests in moist sand.

Mohave Fringe-toed Lizard *Uma scoparia*

A medium-sized (to 114 mm or 4.5"), pale cream to tan, sand-dwelling lizard with a flat body, a flattened tail, and a chisel-like snout. The edges of the toes on the hind feet are fringed with enlarged and pointed scales that expand surface area and therefore increase traction on fine sand. Its cryptic coloration usually closely matches the sand on which it lives. Additional adaptations for living on and burrowing in sand include a chisel-shaped head, countersunk lower jaw, overlapping and interlocking eyelids, flaps over the ear openings, and valves in the nostrils. Markings consist of small orange dots surrounded by black reticulations on the back. Underside is cream, turning to yellow-green during breeding season. A black spot marks each side of the belly and there are black bars under the tail. Its crescent-shaped throat markings, lack of orange bars on the belly, and lack of lines in the back pattern distinguish it from the similar Yuman Desert Fringe-toed Lizard. Restricted to sand dunes and sandy flats, usually with sparse vegetation in Lower Colorado River Desertscrub. A fast running, diurnal, ground dweller that often runs on its hind feet when fleeing. After running a short distance it often wriggles head first into loose sand, thereby rapidly burying itself. Burrows of other animals are also used as refuges. Eats insects and some plant material. Breeds in spring. Lays clutches of 1–5 eggs in spring and summer. Eggs are buried in nests within moist sand.

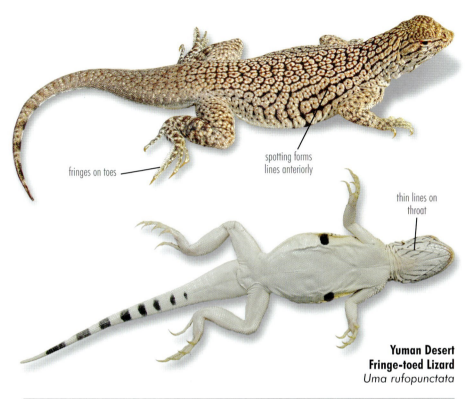

fringes on toes

spotting forms
lines anteriorly

thin lines on
throat

**Yuman Desert
Fringe-toed Lizard**
Uma rufopunctata

fringes on
toes

non-linear spotting

crescents on
throat

**Mohave
Fringe-toed Lizard**
Uma scoparia

Long-tailed Brush Lizard *Urosaurus graciosus*

A small (to 66 mm or 2.6"), pale gray to light brown lizard with gray crossbars that vary from prominent to barely discernable. The throat is often orange or yellow. Males have a blue-green patch on each side of the belly. Its long tail (about twice the body length) and single wide strip of enlarged, keeled scales running down the center of the back distinguish this lizard from the Ornate Tree Lizard. Found in Lower Colorado River Desertscrub and Mohave Desertscrub. Frequently encountered on trees near washes, rivers, or drainages, but also lives on Creosotebushes and other shrubs or trees well out into the flats. Basks on branches where it is well camouflaged. When threatened it will often align itself with a branch or root and remain motionless to avoid detection. Active during the warm daylight hours. Eats insects, spiders, other invertebrates, and some plant material. Lays clutches of 2–10 eggs in spring or summer.

Ornate Tree Lizard *Urosaurus ornatus*

One of our most common and widespread lizards. A small (to 59 mm or 2.3"), gray, tan, or brown lizard with dark gray or brown markings that usually consist of paired, short, and irregularly shaped crossbars. Some are unmarked, or have broken stripes or dashes down the length of the back. Males have a blue patch on each side of the belly and a blue, blue-green, yellow, or orange throat. Females lack belly patches and have a yellow, yellow-green, or orange throat. The top of the head is usually adorned with an ornate pattern of thin dark lines. There are two parallel strips of enlarged, keeled scales that run down the back, separated at the midline by a strip of small granular scales. Its shorter tail (about same length as body) and twin strips of enlarged scales on the back distinguish this lizard from the Long-tailed Brush Lizard. Found in most of Arizona's biotic communities from the low deserts through Petran Montane Conifer Forest. Diurnal. Commonly observed on urban walls, fences, and building exteriors. Natural habitat includes trees, boulders, cliff faces, and rock outcroppings. Eats insects and spiders. Breeds from spring through summer. Lays multiple clutches of 2–16 eggs each, in spring and summer. In urban settings eggs are often laid in water meter boxes, compost heaps, and other moist areas.

Common Side-blotched Lizard *Uta stansburiana*

One of our most common and widespread lizards. A small (to 64 mm or 2.5"), gray-brown to orange-tan lizard with a single dark blue to black blotch on each side of the body just behind the forelimbs. Dorsal markings are variable and can include no pattern, brown blotches, partial striations, or chevron-shaped crossbars. Adult males often have bright turquoise blue speckles on the upper surfaces of the back and tail. The side blotch distinguishes it from Long-tailed Brush Lizard and Ornate Tree Lizard. External ear openings and single side blotch distinguish it from the similar looking Common Lesser Earless Lizard and Elegant Earless Lizard. Found from Lower Colorado River Desertscrub through Interior Chaparral into Plains Grassland. A common lizard that is often seen on the ground under bushes and along the edges of washes in the flats. Also common around boulder piles, rock outcroppings, and steep rocky hillsides. Active year round at low elevations in southwestern and western Arizona. Eats insects, scorpions, spiders, and some plant material. Multiple clutches of 2–5 eggs are laid in spring and summer.

single wide strip of enlarged scales
down middle of back

tail about twice as
long as body

Long-tailed Brush Lizard
Urosaurus graciosus

tail about as long
as body

two parallel strips
of enlarged scales
running down back

Ornate Tree Lizard
Urosaurus ornatus

♂

single
axial blotch

ear
opening

♀

single
axial blotch

Common Side-blotched Lizard
Uta stansburiana

Slevin's Bunchgrass Lizard *Sceloporus slevini*

A small (to 68 mm or 2.7"), brown to yellow-brown lizard with keeled, pointed scales, a light stripe on each upper side, and a wide, gray mid-dorsal stripe. Body relatively long for a *Sceloporus*. The lower sides are often marked with orange, and males sometimes have blue belly patches. Some individuals are boldly patterned and others are relatively plain. Bold patterned animals have bright, crisp-edged stripes connected by dark crescent-shaped blotches on the back and upper sides. Blotches are trimmed with crisp, thin, cream to yellow lines on the back edges. A dark blotch, that sometimes has a light blue center, marks each shoulder. Plain animals lack blotches, the side stripes are lacking or are soft-edged and thin, and the dorsal stripe is gray-brown and much less distinct. The lateral scale rows are arranged horizontally, rather than diagonally upward, distinguishing this lizard from all other *Sceloporus* in Arizona (*see facing page*). Found in communities ranging from grassland to  Petran Subalpine Conifer Forest. Primarily a high elevation (over 2,000 m or 6,500') mountain dweller that lives in and around bunch grass patches in open sunny areas. Also found on rolling hills in ungrazed (or very lightly grazed) grasslands as low as 1,400 m (4,500') in portions of Santa Cruz and Pima Counties. Heavy grazing has been linked to severe declines in some populations. The inner tangles of grass clumps are important retreats from predators and possibly high temperatures. Eats insects and spiders. Mates in April. Lays a clutch of up to 13 eggs in summer.

Striped Plateau Lizard *Sceloporus virgatus*

A small (to 70 mm or 2.75"), dark brown to orange-brown lizard with keeled, pointed scales, a distinct yellow stripe down each side of the back, and a crisp, creamy white stripe down each lower side. Usually two rows of dark blotches on the dorsum. Each dark blotch is often accompanied by a pale gray spot on its inside rear edge. A wide, muted, gray-brown stripe runs down the middle of the back and tail. Underside is usually plain white but occasionally has some dark flecking. A small blue patch is sometimes present on each side of the throat during breeding season. Throat patches are often orange on gravid females. The arrangement of the lateral scale rows distinguish this lizard from Slevin's Bunchgrass Lizard (*see facing page*). The similar looking Southwestern Fence Lizard is larger, has a longer tail, and males have blue belly patches. In Arizona, the Striped Plateau Lizard is known only from the Chiricahua and Peloncillo mountains. Occupies Madrean Evergreen Woodland, Petran  Montane Conifer Forest, and Petran Subalpine Conifer Forest. Most often observed basking or foraging in grassy openings in woodlands or along rocky canyon bottoms. Spends most of its time on the ground, often on or around low rocks and logs. Eats insects and other invertebrates. Mates in April and May. A single clutch of 5–15 eggs is laid in June or July and is timed to coincide with the advent of the monsoon season. After the first monsoon rainstorm of the summer the heads of most females will be muddy from excavating nests and burying their eggs.

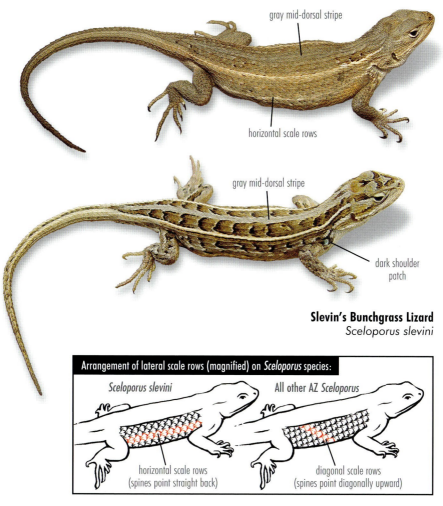

gray mid-dorsal stripe

horizontal scale rows

gray mid-dorsal stripe

dark shoulder patch

Slevin's Bunchgrass Lizard
Sceloporus slevini

Arrangement of lateral scale rows (magnified) on *Sceloporus* species:

Sceloporus slevini

All other AZ *Sceloporus*

horizontal scale rows
(spines point straight back)

diagonal scale rows
(spines point diagonally upward)

dark blotches with a pale spot

diagonal scale rows

Striped Plateau Lizard
Sceloporus virgatus

Common Sagebrush Lizard *Sceloporus graciosus*

A small (to 76 mm or 3"), gray-brown lizard with keeled, pointed scales, and four dark, undulating stripes on the back. A broad, gray-brown stripe marks the mid-dorsum. Often has a rusty patch behind the forelimbs and/or a dark bar on each shoulder. The throat is pale or mottled blue, often with pink and white flecks. Males have dark-edged blue belly patches. Diagonal lateral scale rows distinguish it from Slevin's Bunchgrass Lizard (*see p. 71*). The similar Plateau Lizard and Southwestern Fence Lizard have two blue throat blotches. Lack of side-blotches distinguishes it from the Common Side-blotched Lizard. Distributed from Great Basin Desertscrub to Petran Subalpine Conifer Forest. Diurnal. Found on plains, in low valleys, and on steep slopes, usually in relatively open and sunny areas. Usually observed on the ground near the cover of low bushes, logs, or rocks, but occasionally climbs onto tree trunks. Eats insects, spiders, and scorpions. Mates in May and June. Lays clutches of 2–10 eggs in June and July.

Plateau Lizard *Sceloporus tristichus*

A small (to 80 mm or 3.1"), gray-brown lizard with keeled, pointed, overlapping scales. Often has two light stripes on the back, a gray mid-dorsal stripe, and blotches between stripes. Some specimens have cross bars and lack stripes. Males have prominent, dark-edged, blue belly patches. Belly patches on females are less vivid or are lacking. Distinguishing characteristics include two separated throat blotches, spiny scales, and lack of side blotches. Genetically distinct, but physically indistinguishable from Southwestern Fence Lizard. Soft-edged portions of map indicate ill-defined species boundaries with Southwestern Fence Lizard. The similar looking Striped Plateau Lizard lacks belly markings. Diagonal lateral scale rows distinguish it from Slevin's Bunchgrass Lizard (*see p. 71*). Distributed from Interior Chaparral to Petran Subalpine Conifer Forest. Found in a wide variety of habitats, including grassy plains, shrubby flatlands, foothills, and steep mountain slopes. Diurnal. Forages on the ground, but often seen basking on rock piles, wood piles, boulders, fence posts, fallen logs, and trees. Eats insects, spiders, snails, and small lizards. Breeds in spring and summer. Lays clutches of about 7–10 eggs in spring and summer.

Southwestern Fence Lizard *Sceloporus cowlesi*

A small (to 75 mm or 3"), brown to golden brown lizard with keeled, pointed, overlapping scales. Marked with two light stripes on the back, a gray-brown mid-dorsal stripe, and blotches between stripes. Males have dark-edged blue belly patches. Belly patches are faint or lacking in females. Distinguishing characteristics include two throat blotches, spiny scales, and lack of side blotches. Genetically distinct, but physically indistinguishable from the Plateau Lizard. Soft-edged portions of map indicate ill-defined species boundaries with Plateau Lizard. The similar Striped Plateau Lizard (*S. virgatus*) lacks belly markings. Diagonal lateral scale rows distinguish it from Slevin's Bunchgrass Lizard (*see p. 71*). Found from Semidesert Grassland and Chihuahuan Desertscrub through Petran Montane Conifer Forest. Occupies low valleys, foothills, and grassy plains. In the northern part of its range it can also be found high on steep mountain slopes. Diurnal. Forages on the ground, but often uses rocks, wood piles, fences, and trees for basking and for shelter. Eats insects, spiders, and small lizards. Breeds in spring and summer. Clutches of about 7–10 eggs are laid from May to August.

no prominent
blue patches

dark bar on
shoulder

rusty patch
behind forelimbs

Common Sagebrush Lizard
Sceloporus graciosus

large, pointed
scales

Plateau Lizard
Sceloporus tristichus

no side-blotches

gray mid-dorsal stripe

two throat
blotches

scale rows on sides
are diagonal

two throat
blotches

gray mid-dorsal stripe

scale rows on sides
are diagonal

no side-blotches

Southwestern Fence Lizard
Sceloporus cowlesi

Desert Spiny Lizard *Sceloporus magister*

A large (to 142 mm or 5.6"), heavy-bodied lizard with large, keeled, pointed, overlapping scales. Color is light tan, gray, or yellow-brown, often with dark bars or paired blotches on the back. Some animals lack dorsal blotches. Males have blue-green throat and belly patches. Ventral markings are faint or lacking in females. Males in southern Arizona often have a large purple patch or rows of purple spots on the back. Some central and northern Arizona specimens have bright yellow-orange heads. Black wedges on the shoulders distinguish it from Arizona's smaller *Sceloporus* species. Clark's Spiny Lizard is similar, but has bars on forelimbs. Yarrow's Spiny Lizard differs in that it has a complete collar. Found from Lower Colorado River Desertscrub through Great Basin Conifer Woodland. Often seen on trees, packrat nests, wood piles, fences, and rock piles. When encountered, it will often flee into a crevice or to the opposite side of the tree trunk. Active during the day. Eats ants, beetles, caterpillars, other insects, spiders, centipedes, small lizards, and plants. Often found in male-female pairs. Mates in spring and summer. Lays one or two clutches of 2–12 eggs in spring or summer.

Clark's Spiny Lizard *Sceloporus clarkii*

A large (to 144 mm or 5.6"), stout lizard with keeled, pointed, overlapping scales, dark wedges on the shoulders, and dark bars on the forelimbs. Blue-gray, gray-brown, to sooty gray, often with a blue tint. Crossbars mark the back on juveniles and females. Males have blue patches on the throat and belly which are faint or absent on females. Dark shoulder wedges distinguish it from Arizona's smaller *Sceloporus* species. Desert Spiny Lizard lacks bars on forelimbs, and Yarrow's Spiny Lizard has a complete collar. Found from desertscrub communities up into Madrean Evergreen Woodland and Great Basin Conifer Woodland. Diurnal. Strongly associated with trees, but also uses rock piles and outcroppings. When threatened, it usually flees to the opposite side of the tree trunk, climbing up and out of reach. Eats beetles, ants, caterpillars, wasps, other insects, spiders, and some plant material. Mates in spring. Usually lays a clutch of up to 28 eggs at the onset of the monsoon. May occasionally lay a second, smaller clutch.

Yarrow's Spiny Lizard *Sceloporus jarrovii*

A medium-sized (to 105 mm or 4.1") lizard with keeled, pointed, overlapping scales, a broad black collar, and a net-like pattern on the torso. A thin white line edges the rear margin of the collar. The net-like torso pattern is created by pale scales with thick black edges. The pale centers of these scales reflect tints of copper, pink, green, and blue. The top of the head is dark gray. The tail is notably more spiny than the body. Males have blue throat and belly patches. Blue ventral markings are faint on females. The complete collar distinguishes it from Arizona's other *Sceloporus*. Inhabits Madrean Evergreen Woodland, Petran Montane Conifer Forest, and Petran Subalpine Conifer Forest. The Santa Catalina Mountains population is introduced. A diurnal rock-dweller that frequents rock slides, cliffs, and bouldery canyon bottoms, often near creek beds. Only rarely climbs trees. This lizard is active year-round, but winter basking and foraging is limited to relatively warm sunny days. Eats ants, wasps, beetles, caterpillars, grasshoppers, other insects, and spiders. Live-bearing. Mates in fall and gives birth to 2–14 young, usually in June.

dark wedges on
shoulders

no bars on
forelimbs

Desert Spiny Lizard
Sceloporus magister

dark bars
on forelimbs

Clark's Spiny Lizard
Sceloporus clarkii

tail more spiny
than body

collar
complete

no bars on
forelimbs

Yarrow's Spiny Lizard
Sceloporus jarrovii

Texas Horned Lizard *Phrynosoma cornutum*

A medium-sized (to 130 mm or 5"), particularly flat, and broad lizard. Long horn-like scales protrude from the back of the head. The two central head spikes are longer than the others. Isolated pointed scales project from the back, and two fringes of enlarged, pointed scales line each lower side. Rust to yellow-brown with a crisp, white dorsal stripe. Dark spots and neck patches outlined in yellow mark the back. Prominent dark stripes radiating from the eyes distinguish this lizard from all other Arizona horned lizards. Inhabits low valleys and gentle bajadas, usually with loose sandy or gravelly soil within Chihuahuan Desertscrub and Semidesert Grassland. When threatened it often remains still, relying on crypsis for defense. Sometimes squirts blood from its eyes when threatened or captured. Drinks by arching its back and lowering its head during rain, allowing the water to run down its body to its mouth. Diurnal. Spends nights in burrows or buried in sandy soil and emerges after sunrise to bask and forage. Usually seeks shelter in the shade of shrubs during the hot part of the day and emerges again in late afternoon. Eats ants and other insects. Mates in spring. Lays clutches of up to about 30 eggs from May to August.

Flat-tailed Horned Lizard *Phrynosoma mcallii*

PROTECTED A small (to 87 mm or 3.4"), particularly flat, and broad lizard with a long flat tail and no external ear openings. Long horn-like scales protrude from the back of the head. The two central head spikes are much longer than the others. Coloration is tan to reddish brown and closely matches the sand on which the lizard lives. Dark spots and isolated pointed scales adorn the back. Two fringes of enlarged, pointed scales line each lower side. The only Arizona horned lizard with a dark mid-dorsal stripe. Inhabits hard-packed sandy flats and low dunes in Lower Colorado River Desertscrub. Burrows into the sand to avoid the heat of the day and cold nights. When threatened it often remains motionless, relying on crypsis to avoid detection. Acquires most of its water from its food. Eats ants and occasionally beetles and other insects. Mates in April and May. Lays clutches of up to 10 eggs in May and June. This lizard has a very limited range in Arizona and is threatened by off-road vehicles, urban sprawl, and the spread of agriculture.

Desert Horned Lizard *Phrynosoma platyrhinos*

A medium-sized (to 95 mm or 3.75"), particularly flat, and broad lizard. Long horn-like scales protrude from the back of the head. Various shades of brown overall, with highlights of orange or salmon along the lower edges of the body. Coloration often matches the soil on which the lizard is found. Almost always has a pair of dark blotches on the neck. On the back are scattered large, pointed scales and irregular dark blotches. The bases of the head spikes are not in contact with one another. There is but a single fringe of enlarged, pointed scales on each side. Found in Sonoran Desertscrub, Mohave Desertscrub, and Great Basin Desertscrub. Usually encountered in flat, open areas with sparse vegetation, but also inhabits rocky bajadas and hillsides. More likely to run than most horned lizards, although it often stops after a short sprint. Shelters in existing burrows or buries itself in sandy soil. Eats ants, other insects, and some plant material. Lays one or two clutches of up to 16 eggs from May to August.

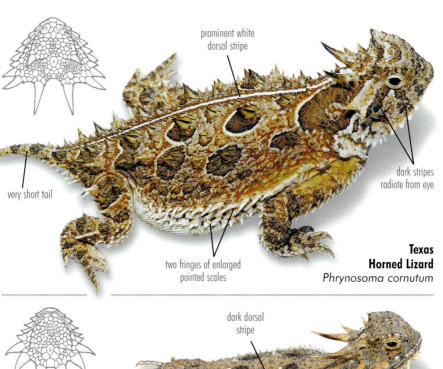

prominent white
dorsal stripe

dark stripes
radiate from eye

very short tail

two fringes of enlarged
pointed scales

**Texas
Horned Lizard**
Phrynosoma cornutum

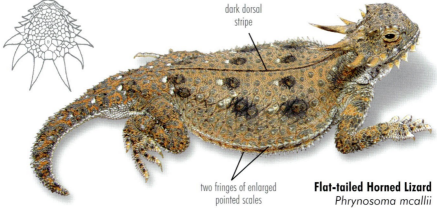

dark dorsal
stripe

two fringes of enlarged
pointed scales

Flat-tailed Horned Lizard
Phrynosoma mcallii

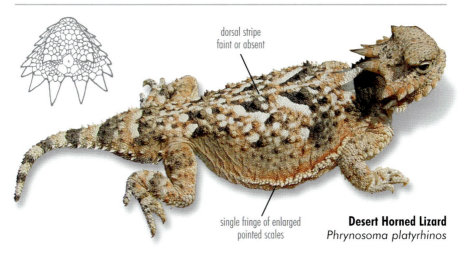

dorsal stripe
faint or absent

single fringe of enlarged
pointed scales

Desert Horned Lizard
Phrynosoma platyrhinos

Regal Horned Lizard *Phrynosoma solare*

A medium-sized (to 117 mm or 4.6"), particularly flat, and broad lizard. A prominent crown of flattened horn-like scales radiates from the sides and back of the head. The four central horns are roughly equal in length and their bases touch, distinguishing this lizard from other Arizona horned lizards. Pointed scales protrude from the back and a single row of enlarged, pointed scales fringes the lower edge of the body. Reddish brown, tan, or gray in color, often matching the substrate. The central portion of the back is usually lighter in color than the sides. A faint, light mid-dorsal stripe is sometimes present. Two dark blotches often mark the top of the neck. Found in valleys and on rocky bajadas within Arizona Upland Desertscrub, Chihuahuan Desertscrub, and Semidesert Grassland. Active year-round, but winter activity is restricted to warm, sunny days. This lizard sometimes squirts blood from its eyes when threatened or captured. Eats ants, small beetles, and other insects. Lays a clutch of up to 33 eggs in summer. Eggs are deposited in a chamber at the end of a tunnel dug in loose soil.

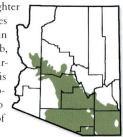

Greater Short-horned Lizard *Phrynosoma hernandesi*

A medium-sized (to 125 mm or 4.9"), particularly flat, and broad lizard. Short, stubby, horn-like scales project from the back of the head. A broad gap separates the two central horns, distinguishing this lizard from other Arizona horned lizards. A single row of pointed protruding scales fringes each lower side of the body, and small, spike-like scales are scattered across the back. The tan, yellowish, reddish-brown, or gray body usually matches the substrate. Two large, dark blotches mark the neck and dark, irregular blotches or cross-bars mark the back. A cold tolerant lizard found in communities ranging from Semidesert Grassland through Petran Subalpine Conifer Forest. Usually found in open sunlit areas within mountainous terrain, but also occupies flat shrublands and rolling hills. A ground dweller that usually remains motionless when encountered, relying on crypsis to avoid detection. This lizard sometimes squirts blood from its eyes when threatened or captured. Ants comprise the bulk of its diet, but it also eats beetles and other insects. Mates from March to May. Gives birth to up to 48 young per clutch in summer.

Round-tailed Horned Lizard *Phrynosoma modestum*

A small (to 70 mm or 2.75"), particularly flat, and broad lizard. Short, widely separated horn-like scales protrude from the back of the head. There are no distinct fringes on the lower sides of the body, distinguishing this lizard from all other Arizona horned lizards. The back has relatively few spines, and the tail is thin and round in cross-section. The body is pale gray, pinkish, yellow, tan, or blue-gray and usually matches the substrate. Coloration of individual lizards can change to more closely match substrate and to aid thermoregulation. Dark bands on the tail. Dark coloration on the sides of the neck, body, and behind each hind limb resemble shadows and aid crypsis. When encountered it often remains still and hunches its back. In this posture, the lizard looks remarkably like a small rock which may help it avoid detection. A ground dweller usually found on gravelly bajadas, low slopes, and foothills within Chihuahuan Desertscrub and Semidesert Grass-land. Usually active in the morning and late afternoon, but also occasionally active at night. Eats primarily ants, but also termites, beetles, and other insects. Clutches of up to 19 eggs are laid from May to July.

light area on top
center of back

bases of
horns touch

single fringe of
enlarged scales

Regal Horned Lizard
Phrynosoma solare

single fringe of enlarged
pointed scales

Greater Short-horned Lizard
Phrynosoma hernandesi

skinny
round tail

no distinct fringe

Round-tailed Horned Lizard
Phrynosoma modestum

Chihuahuan Spotted Whiptail *Aspidoscelis exsanguis*

A slim, medium-sized (to 100 mm or 3.9"), brown or reddish brown lizard with six (rarely seven) stripes and a long, thin, brown to olive-brown tail. Distinguished by faded stripes (in adults), relatively large numbers of cream spots on the back and sides, and bright yellow spots atop the rump and hind legs. Active during the day in canyons, rocky slopes, and riparian corridors within Semidesert Grassland, Madrean Evergreen Woodland, and lower elevations of Petran Montane Conifer Forest. A diurnal lizard that forages for termites, beetles, other insects, spiders, and scorpions by digging in leaf litter or under rocks and logs. Clutches of 1–6 eggs are laid in summer. Parthenogenetic (an asexual, all-female lineage, in which hatchlings are clones of the mother).

Gila Spotted Whiptail *Aspidoscelis flagellicauda*

A slim, medium-sized (to 99 mm or 3.9"), brown to black lizard with a long, olive-brown to blue-brown tail and six yellow stripes. Distinguished by distinct striping on neck, relatively few light spots on the body, and usually two enlarged preanals (*see page 56*). Actively forages during the day in canyons, riparian corridors, and on slopes in communities ranging from Semidesert Grassland to Petran Montane Conifer Forest. Often seen mid-morning in sunny areas along the banks of creeks and rivers. Eats insects and spiders. Lays 2–6 eggs in June or July. Parthenogenetic (an asexual, all-female lineage, in which hatchlings are clones of the mother).

Sonoran Spotted Whiptail *Aspidoscelis sonorae*

A slim, small to medium (to 89 mm or 3.5"), brown or black lizard with a long brown to olive-brown tail and six yellow to cream stripes. Distinguished by distinct striping on neck, relatively few spots on the body, and usually three enlarged preanals (*see page 56*). Found on hills, in canyons, riparian corridors, and low valleys within Semidesert Grassland, Madrean Evergreen Woodland, and Petran Montane Conifer Forest. A diurnal lizard, usually most active in morning and late afternoon. Eats termites and other invertebrates. Lays clutches of up to seven eggs. Parthenogenetic (an asexual, all-female lineage, in which hatchlings are clones of the mother).

New Mexico Whiptail *Aspidoscelis neomexicana*

NON-NATIVE A slim, small (to 82 mm or 3.25"), brown to black lizard with a long, blue tipped, gray-green tail and seven light stripes. The only whiptail in Arizona with a wavy mid-dorsal stripe. There are spots in the dark areas on the back and upper sides. A small population, probably an introduction, was discovered in 1998 near Puerco Ruins visitor site in Petrified Forest National Park. This population lives on a shrubby, sandy floodplain in Plains Grassland. Usually most active mid morning and late afternoon, avoiding the hottest part of the day. Hibernates in a self-dug burrow. Eats insects. Lays one or two clutches of 1–4 eggs each in June and July. Parthenogenetic (an asexual, all-female lineage, in which hatchlings are clones of the mother).

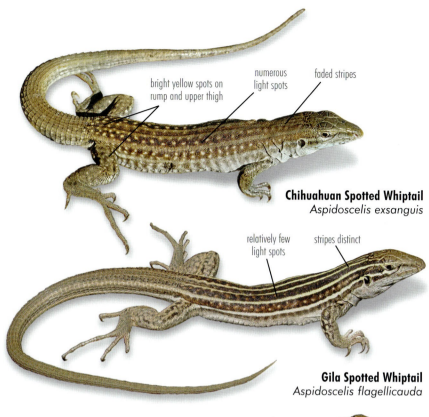

bright yellow spots on
rump and upper thigh

numerous
light spots

faded stripes

Chihuahuan Spotted Whiptail
Aspidoscelis exsanguis

relatively few
light spots

stripes distinct

Gila Spotted Whiptail
Aspidoscelis flagellicauda

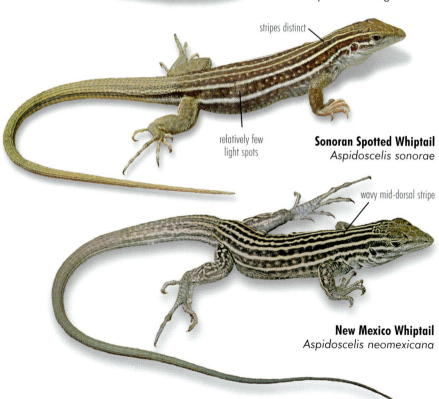

stripes distinct

relatively few
light spots

Sonoran Spotted Whiptail
Aspidoscelis sonorae

wavy mid-dorsal stripe

New Mexico Whiptail
Aspidoscelis neomexicana

Desert Grassland Whiptail *Aspidoscelis uniparens*

A slim, small (to 86 mm or 3.3"), dark brown lizard with six light stripes on the back. Occasionally has a partial mid-dorsal (seventh) stripe. The long, thin tail is muted blue to olive. No light spots on the body. Usually has three enlarged, rounded preanals (*see page 56*) distinguishing it from the Plateau Striped Whiptail. Active mornings and late afternoons. Found in valleys and on slopes within Semidesert Grassland and Interior Chaparral. Follows drainages into the woodlands. An active forager that eats termites and other insects. Lays two or three clutches of 1–4 eggs each. Parthenogenetic (an asexual, all-female lineage, in which hatchlings are clones of the mother).

Plateau Striped Whiptail *Aspidoscelis velox*

A slim, small (to 85 mm or 3.3"), dark brown to black lizard with six or seven light stripes and a light blue tail. When present, the mid-dorsal (seventh) stripe is muted or discontinuous and is often slightly undulating. Occasionally has a few faint, soft-edged spots in the dark areas. Usually has four or more enlarged, angular preanals (*see page 56*) distinguishing it from the similar Desert Grassland Whiptail. Found in Plains and Great Basin Grassland, Great Basin Conifer Woodland, and Petran Montane Conifer Forest. This diurnal lizard spends most of its waking hours on the move, actively foraging for insects and spiders. Lays 3–5 eggs in summer. Parthenogenetic (an asexual, all-female lineage, in which hatchlings are clones of the mother).

Arizona Striped Whiptail *Aspidoscelis arizonae*

A small (to 72 mm or 2.8"), gracile, brown to reddish brown lizard with seven light yellow stripes (mid-dorsal stripe often diminished) and a long, thin, bright blue tail. Distinguished by pale blue coloration on face, feet, and underside, lack of spots, and usually 2–3 enlarged preanals (*see page 56*). The similar Pai Striped Whiptail has only six complete stripes. Found in low valleys and sandy flats within Semidesert Grassland. Diurnal. Most active in the morning. Forages for insects, spiders, centipedes, and small lizards by digging around the bases of bushes and under surface debris. Mates in spring. Lays one or two clutches of 1–3 eggs each in late spring or early summer.

Pai Striped Whiptail *Aspidoscelis pai*

A small (to 85 mm or 3.4"), gracile, brown to reddish brown lizard with six light yellow stripes. Tail is long, thin, and bright blue. Some have an incomplete or very thin mid-dorsal (seventh) stripe. Distinguishing characteristics include pale blue coloration on face, feet, and underside, a lack of spots, and usually 2–3 enlarged preanals (*see page 56*). The similar looking Arizona Striped Whiptail has seven complete stripes. Found primarily in Plains and Great Basin Grassland, but also occurs in Interior Chaparral, Great Basin Conifer Woodland, and Petran Montane Conifer Forest. A diurnal lizard that is most active in the morning. Forages by digging in leaf litter and under rocks and logs in search of insects, spiders, centipedes, and hatchling lizards. Mates in spring. Lays one or two clutches of 1–3 eggs each in late spring or early summer.

no spots

muted blue-green tail

Desert Grassland Whiptail
Aspidoscelis uniparens

blue tail

no spots

Plateau Striped Whiptail
Aspidoscelis velox

7 stripes

blue tail

no spots

blue
coloration

Arizona Striped Whiptail
Aspidoscelis arizonae

6 complete stripes

blue tail

blue
coloration

no spots

Pai Striped Whiptail
Aspidoscelis pai

Red-backed Whiptail *Aspidoscelis xanthonota*

A medium-sized (to about 114 mm or 4.5"), slim lizard with an orange-red tint on the back and a long thin tail. Orange-red coloration is restricted to the top of the lower back and does not extend onto the sides. There are light spots or blotches on the back, sides, and hind limbs. The face, sides of the body, neck, and feet are often tinted blue or blue-green. Distinguished by a lack of stripes in adults. Young are striped. The similar looking Tiger Whiptail has dark mottling or reticulations on the sides and chest. Inhabits mountains within Arizona Upland Desertscrub. Frequents broad, rocky canyon bottoms and follows drainages out a short distance onto steep bajadas. A diurnal lizard that is often seen in the vicinity of springs or tinajas. Eats termites, ants, other insects, and spiders. Reproduces sexually. Lays clutches of up to 10 eggs each in summer.

Canyon Spotted Whiptail *Aspidoscelis burti*

A large (to 140 mm or 5.5") lizard with a long, thin, orange tail, and red-orange coloration on the head and neck. Juveniles and small adults have six (rarely seven) crisp, light stripes on the body. As they age, the stripes begin to break up into light spots. Some large adults are spotted and lack stripes entirely. This is the largest whiptail lizard in the United States. The similar looking Red-backed Whiptail is smaller and usually does not have orange-red coloration on the head and neck. The similar looking Sonoran Spotted Whiptail is much smaller, does not completely lose its stripes with age, and usually has less orange coloration on the tail, hind limbs, and feet. Inhabits Semidesert Grassland and Madrean Evergreen Woodland. A diurnal lizard that is usually encountered in canyon bottoms within mountainous terrain. Also inhabits washes, riparian corridors, and low valley bottoms, usually near streams or temporary water. Eats insects and spiders. Reproduces sexually. Lays one or two clutches of up to 10 eggs each in summer.

Tiger Whiptail *Aspidoscelis tigris*

A medium-sized (to 110 mm or 4.3"), slim, orange-brown to gray-brown lizard with a long, thin tail and dark mottling on the back and sides. Mottling is usually darkest and most distinct near and above the forelimbs. Faint stripes are sometimes present on the back but they often fade into the background with age. On males the throat and chest are either mottled with black or are solid black, distinguishing it from other whiptails. Young have more distinct striping and blue tails. Found in the desertscrub communities, Semidesert Grassland, and lower reaches of Interior Chaparral. Occupies a wide variety of habitats including wind blown sand dunes, Creosotebush flats, broad sandy washes, rocky canyons, bajadas, hillsides, and sagebrush plateaus. A very active diurnal lizard. Spends most of its waking hours on the move, foraging on the surface and digging for food in leaf litter and under plants, rocks, and debris. Eats termites, grasshoppers, other insects, spiders, scorpions, and small lizards. Mates in spring and summer. One or more clutches of 1–5 eggs are laid in spring and summer.

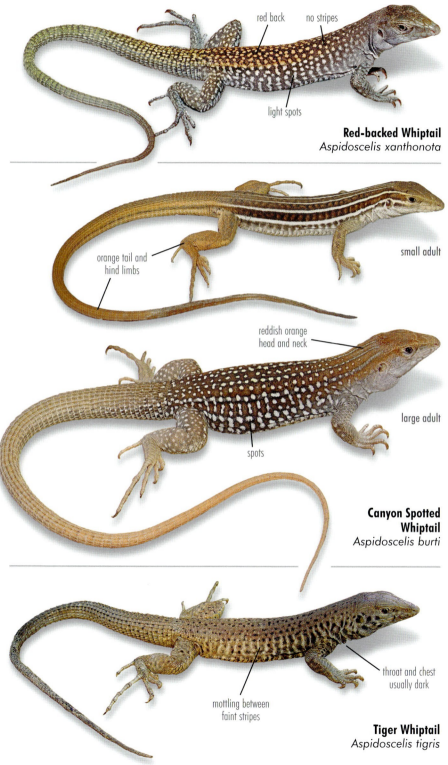

red back　　no stripes

light spots

Red-backed Whiptail
Aspidoscelis xanthonota

orange tail and
hind limbs

small adult

reddish orange
head and neck

large adult

spots

**Canyon Spotted
Whiptail**
Aspidoscelis burti

throat and chest
usually dark

mottling between
faint stripes

Tiger Whiptail
Aspidoscelis tigris

Mountain Skink *Eumeces callicephalus*

A small (to 76 mm or 3"), shiny, copper, golden brown, or olive-brown lizard with relatively small limbs and a bright blue tail. Adults retain blue coloration on tail, distinguishing it from other Arizona skinks. A dark, wide stripe runs along each side from the eye to the hind limbs. A thin pale line sometimes borders the upper edge of the dark, wide stripe. Some specimens, particularly juveniles and young adults, have a pale Y shape on top of the head. Adult males may develop red coloration on the lips. Inhabits Madrean Evergreen Woodland and upper reaches of Semidesert Grassland. Often found under rocks and logs along canyon bottoms. Active during the day, but activity is usually restricted to moist areas around the cover of rock piles, fallen logs, leaf litter, and dense grass. Rarely strays into dry, open areas. Eats insects and spiders. Both egg laying and live birth have been documented in Arizona. The female stays in the nest to care for the eggs, and clutch size ranges from 3–6.

Many-lined Skink *Eumeces multivirgatus*

A small (to 76 mm or 3"), shiny, tan to brown lizard with relatively small limbs and a very long, thick tail. A thin pale cream stripe lines each side of the back. Multiple dark brown stripes on the body contrast with adjacent light tan stripes. Stripes are faint or absent on some specimens. The long tail (when not regenerated) and numerous and varied stripes distinguish this skink from other Arizona skinks. Young are darker brown and have blue tails. Males may develop orangish red coloration on the lips during breeding season. Found in communities ranging from Plains and Great Basin Grassland through Petran Montane Conifer Forest. Inhabits canyons in mountainous terrain, open grassy hillsides, meadows, low valleys, and plateaus. Most frequently found in moist areas under rocks or logs. Eats insects. Lays eggs in shallow nests excavated in moist soil under rocks, logs, or other surface objects. A clutch of 3–9 eggs is laid in late spring or summer. The female stays in the nest to brood the eggs.

Western Skink *Eumeces skiltonianus*

A small (to 86 mm or 3.4"), shiny, dark brown to reddish brown lizard with relatively small limbs and a dull, blue-gray to gray tail. A light cream or tan stripe runs along each upper side extending from the snout, over the eye, along the edge of the back, and onto the tail. A second light cream or tan stripe extends from the upper lip, along each lower side, and onto the tail. Often has orangish red coloration on the chin and sides of head. Young are darker brown to black with bright cream to yellow stripes and a bright blue tail. The similar looking Many-lined Skink has more numerous and varied stripes than the Western Skink. Found along rocky canyon bottoms and on steep, rocky slopes and open sunlit hillsides within Petran Montane Conifer Forest and Petran Subalpine Conifer Forest. Active during the day, but most activity takes place under the cover of rocks, logs, or leaf litter. Eats insects and spiders. Lays a clutch of 2–10 eggs in an underground nest during summer. Female stays in the nest to watch over the eggs.

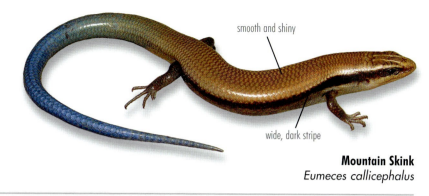

smooth and shiny

wide, dark stripe

Mountain Skink
Eumeces callicephalus

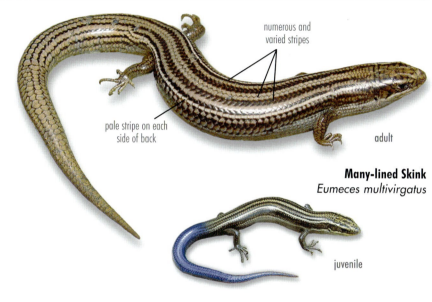

numerous and
varied stripes

pale stripe on each
side of back

adult

Many-lined Skink
Eumeces multivirgatus

juvenile

adult

juvenile

Western Skink
Eumeces skiltonianus

Gilbert's Skink *Eumeces gilberti*

A medium-sized (to 114 mm or 4.5"), shiny gray, tan, or olive lizard with a stocky body, relatively small limbs, and a thick tail. Young are dark brown with four light stripes on the body and a pink tail. Stripes fade with age and adults are uniformly colored. Some adults develop red or orange coloration on the head. Distinguished from other Arizona skinks by its lack of markings and pink-tailed young. Found in a wide variety of communi-ties, including Arizona Upland Desertscrub, Interior Chaparral, Great Basin Conifer Woodland, and Petran Montane Conifer Forest. Presence in desertscrub is generally confined to riparian corridors shaded by large trees. In higher elevation communities it inhabits moist rocky canyons, boulder fields, and steep, shaded slopes. Shelters under rocks, leaf litter, logs, and other surface debris. This secretive lizard is active during the day but most activity occurs under cover. Eats insects and spiders. Lays a clutch of 3–9 eggs in an underground nest during summer.

Great Plains Skink *Eumeces obsoletus*

A large (to 133 mm or 5.6"), shiny tan, gray, or olive lizard with a stocky body, a thick tail, and short limbs. A dark crescent on the rear edge of each scale creates a net-like pattern over the body, distinguishing this skink from Gilbert's Skink. The dark crescents occasionally merge together forming blotchy areas or rough lengthwise lines. The tail and limbs are often tinted yellow to orange-yellow, and there are usually orange spots on the lower sides. The dorsum often has a light pinkish or mauve cast. Young are black with bright blue tails and prominent white spots on the sides of the face. Inhabits Semidesert Grassland, 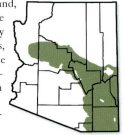Interior Chaparral, woodland, and lower reaches of Petran Montane Conifer Forest. Found from low valleys through foothills and rocky canyons up into mountains. Shelters in moist areas under rocks, logs, leaf litter, or in burrows. A secretive lizard that spends most of its time under cover, but is occasionally encountered abroad on mild mornings, overcast days, and following rain. Nocturnal activity has been observed in Arizona. Eats insects, spiders, snails, and small lizards. Lays a clutch of 7–24 eggs in an underground nest during spring or summer. Female stays in the nest and guards the eggs.

Madrean Alligator Lizard *Elgaria kingii*

A large (to 140 mm or 5.5"), shiny, long-bodied lizard with relatively small limbs and a long, thick tail. The back and belly are armored with stiff, rectangular, plate-like scales. A soft fold of skin on each side allows the body to expand for breathing. Coloration is gray or tan with chocolate or reddish brown crossbars that have dark posterior edges. Often has crisp white markings on the sides of the face. Young have crisp, nearly black band-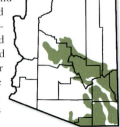ing on the body and tail and dark coloration on the limbs, feet, and lower sides. Occupies low valleys, rolling foothills, and steep mountain slopes in communities ranging from Semidesert Grassland through Petran Montane Conifer Forest. Active during the day and evening. This ground dweller is often found foraging in leaf litter or under rock piles, rat nests, fallen logs, or dead plants. Seems to be most abundant in wooded canyons or along drainages. Eats insects, spiders, and scorpions. Presumably a fall breeder. Lays up to 15 eggs in late spring or early summer.

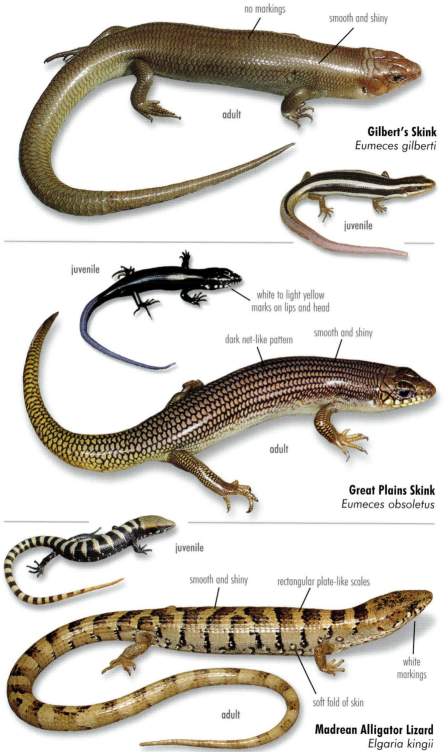

no markings

smooth and shiny

adult

Gilbert's Skink
Eumeces gilberti

juvenile

juvenile

white to light yellow
marks on lips and head

dark net-like pattern

smooth and shiny

adult

Great Plains Skink
Eumeces obsoletus

juvenile

smooth and shiny

rectangular plate-like scales

white
markings

soft fold of skin

adult

Madrean Alligator Lizard
Elgaria kingii

Western Banded Gecko *Coleonyx variegatus*

A small (to 76 mm or 3"), pinkish tan lizard with dark reddish brown crossbars or reticulations. Young usually have distinct crossbars that break up into reticulations as the animal ages. Adults in southeastern Arizona tend to retain juvenile pattern. Skin is soft, translucent, and covered in small, granular scales. The pupils are vertical. The tail is 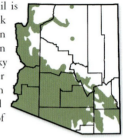 banded, and is plump in well-fed individuals. Moveable eyelids, lack of tubercles, and lack of toe pads distinguish it from Mediterranean House Gecko. Primarily a resident of the desertscrub communities in habitats ranging from dry, wind-blown sand dunes to steep, rocky mountainsides. Often undulates its tail in a sinuous, cat-like manner when threatened. The tail is easily lost and regenerated. Often squeaks when captured. An almost exclusively nocturnal ground dweller that eats insects and spiders. Lays one or more clutches of 1–2 eggs in spring and summer.

Mediterranean House Gecko *Hemidactylus turcicus*

NON-NATIVE A small (to 60 mm or 2.4"), peach or light pinkish tan lizard with dark reticulations, spots, or crossbars and translucent skin. The  pupils are vertical. Whitish tubercles on the back, prominent toe pads, and lidless eyes distinguish it from Western Banded Gecko. An introduced Mediterranean and west Asian lizard that is restricted to urban areas in Arizona. Toe pads and claws enable it to climb upside down on ceilings and on vertical walls. Commonly seen at night near lights on buildings. Waits to ambush insects attracted to the light. May squeak when captured. Might breed year-round in Arizona. Lays 1–3 clutches per year, each consisting of two hard-shelled eggs.

Bezy's Night Lizard *Xantusia bezyi*

A small (to 70 mm or 2.75"), olive to yellow-brown lizard with bold blotches or spots on the back and tail. Scales on the back are small and granular. Scales on belly and tail are large and rectangular. Head  scales are large and plate-like. Lidless orange to red eyes with vertical pupils. Head and body are somewhat flattened. This lizard is a secretive crevice dweller that lives in large rock outcroppings, cliff faces, and boulder fields within Arizona Upland Desertscrub, Interior Chaparral, and woodland communities. Rarely seen away from the safety of crevices during the day. Eats insects and spiders. Mates in spring and gives birth to 1–3 young in summer.

Desert Night Lizard *Xantusia vigilis*

A small (to 57 mm or 2.25"), olive-gray to yellow-brown lizard with dark flecks or speckles on the back and tail. The scales on the back are small and granular. Scales on belly and tail are large and rectangular.  Head scales are large and plate-like. The eyes are lidless and the pupils are vertical. Inhabits foothills and mountain slopes in communities ranging from desertscrub to Interior Chaparral. Usually found in or under plant debris such as dead agaves and prickly pear cactus, but also found in rock crevices. This secretive lizard rarely emerges from cover during the day. Eats insects, spiders, and other invertebrates. Mates in spring. Gives birth to 1–3 young in summer.

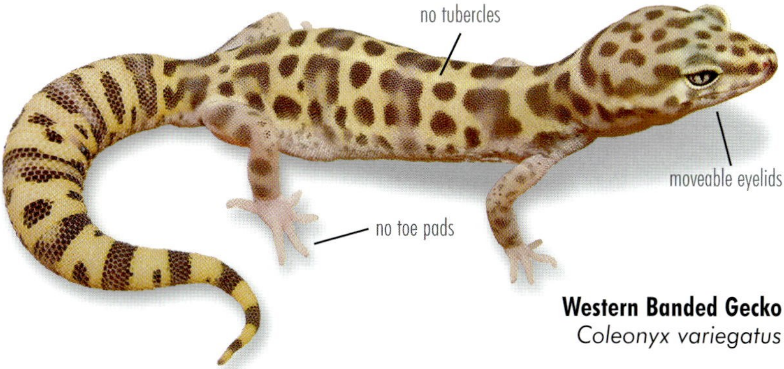

no tubercles

moveable eyelids

no toe pads

Western Banded Gecko
Coleonyx variegatus

tubercles on back

no eyelids

toe pads

Mediterranean House Gecko
Hemidactylus turcicus

no eyelids

fold of skin

Bezy's Night Lizard
Xantusia bezyi

no eyelids

fold of skin

Desert Night Lizard
Xantusia vigilis

Gila Monster *Heloderma suspectum*

VENOMOUS • PROTECTED The largest (to 356 mm or 14") native lizard in the United States and a member of the only family of dangerously venomous lizards in the world (Helodermatidae). Stout bodied with a large head, stocky limbs and a short, fat tail. Black bands or reticulations on an orange, yellow, or pinkish body. Three to five (usually four) black bands on the tail. Snout and sides of face are usually black. Hard, round, bead-like scales cover the upper surfaces of the head, body, limbs, and tail. Belly scales are flat and rectangular. Two forms are currently recognized and both occur in Arizona. Banded Gila Monsters are generally found in northwestern and western Arizona. Reticulate Gila Monsters are generally found in central and southeastern Arizona. Both forms are banded as juveniles. Pattern varies geographically (is not dichotomous) and both banded and reticulated specimens are sometimes found outside of the geographic ranges described above. Primarily a resident of desertscrub communities but also occupies Semidesert Grassland, Interior Chaparral, and is occasionally found in woodland. Often encountered on rocky bajadas, hillsides, and in mountainous terrain. Spends most of its life underground in burrows, packrat nests, or rock crevices. Total surface activity may add up to three or four weeks per year. Active at any time of the year, with a peak in spring. Diurnal in spring and fall and mostly nocturnal in summer. Winter activity is limited to basking on sunny days. Usually overwinters in shelters on south-facing, rocky hillsides. Slow moving, and defensive only when frightened or harassed. Venom is secreted by glands in the lower jaw and is delivered via grooves in the teeth by chewing. Although envenomations are extremely painful they are rarely, if ever, fatal to humans who receive appropriate medical care. An efficient nest raider, the Gila Monster feeds on the eggs of birds and reptiles, nestling birds and mammals, small lizards, and carrion. Four or five meals may allow it to store enough fat in its tail to sustain the lizard for a year. Mates in spring and early summer. Males aggressively fight each other for access to receptive females in matches that can last for several hours. Females usually reproduce only every other year and lay a clutch of up to 12 eggs in July or August. Hatchling Gila Monsters have only been observed in the spring. Captive specimens have lived for up to 25 years. The first venomous reptile to be protected in the United States. It is illegal to handle, collect, or kill a Gila Monster throughout its entire range in the United States and Mexico.

Reticulate Gila Monster

bead like scales

Banded Gila Monster

plump tail

plump tail

Gila Monster
Heloderma suspectum

*S*nakes, together with lizards and amphisbaenians, comprise the order Squamata *(see p. 56)*. Some lizard families, such as Helodermatidae (Gila Monsters and Beaded Lizards) and Varanidae (Monitors), are more closely related to snakes than they are to other lizards. In other words, snakes are but a group of highly specialized lizards.

Although limb reduction has evolved many times in Squamata, snakes have taken limbless-ness and body elongation to its extreme. All snakes are legless and most lack even vestiges of bony limb structures. All snakes also lack external ear openings and moveable eyelids. Slender form has resulted in changes in the organization of internal organs. Snakes have nearly lost their left lung and other paired organs are arranged fore and aft, rather than side by side. Snakes rely extensively on chemoreception, gathering particles from the environment with their tongues and "smelling" them using a sensory organ on the roof of the mouth.

Although snakes are but a single group of lizard, Arizona is home to 52 species, more than all other Arizona "lizards" combined. Of 17 snake families worldwide, five are found in Arizona. Leptotyphlopidae is a small group of snakes that is very distantly related to most other living snakes. Our Arizona representatives, Threadsnakes *(p. 96)*, have reduced eyes and superficially resemble shiny, almost metallic earthworms. Elapidae have fixed, hollow fangs that deliver a primarily neurotoxic venom. Elapidae includes mambas, taipans, sea snakes, and cobras, as well as our own Sonoran Coralsnake *(p. 98)*. Viperidae includes all rattlesnakes *(pp. 124-133)*. Retractable, hollow fangs, a rattle, and heat sensing pits on the sides of the face make these serpents difficult to misidentify. Most of our snakes belong to Colubridae *(pp. 98–123)*, a large and variable family that probably does not represent a single evolutionary group. Colubrids are generally harmless although some have mildly toxic venom. None in Arizona pose a serious threat to human safety.

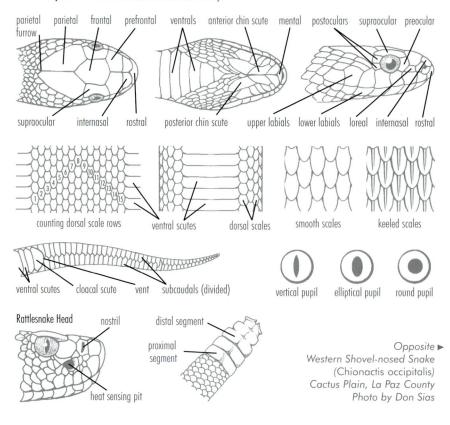

Opposite ▶
Western Shovel-nosed Snake
(Chionactis occipitalis)
Cactus Plain, La Paz County
Photo by Don Sias

New Mexico Threadsnake *Leptotyphlops dissectus*

A small (to 300 mm or 11.8") snake that superficially resembles a thin, shiny earthworm. Both the head and tail are blunt. Tail with a small terminal spine. Eyes visible as dark blemishes beneath the scales. Pinkish to mauve in color with a silvery sheen. Ventral scales are roughly the same size as the dorsal scales. Presence of supraoculars distinguishes this snake from the Western Threadsnake. Found in communities ranging from Chihuahuan Desertscrub and Semidesert Grassland up into foothills of Madrean Evergreen Woodland. This snake spends most of its time underground and is most  often encountered beneath surface objects. Sometimes found crawling on the surface at dusk or during the night. Feeds primarily on ants and termites, but also eats other larval insects, harvestmen, millipedes, solpugids, and spiders. Small owls capture and release these snakes in their nests, where they presumably feed on owl ectoparasites. Probably mates in spring and lays 1–8 eggs underground in midsummer. Females tend their eggs and sometimes nest communally. Hatching probably occurs in August or September.

Western Threadsnake *Leptotyphlops humilis*

A small (to 389 mm or 15") snake that superficially resembles a shiny, thin earthworm. Both the head and tail are blunt. Tail has a small terminal spine. Eyes visible as dark blemishes beneath the scales. Pinkish to mauve in color with a silvery sheen. Ventral scales are roughly the same size as dorsal scales. Absence of supraoculars distinguishes this snake from the New Mexico Threadsnake. Found from desertscrub communities, through  Semidesert Grassland, up into Interior Chaparral. Primarily nocturnal. This snake spends most of its time underground where it feeds mainly on adult and larval ants and termites. Also eats other larval insects, centipedes, millipedes, whipscorpions, and spiders. Small owls capture and release these snakes in their nests, where they presumably feed on owl ectoparasites. Lays 2–8 eggs underground in July or August. Nests of eggs are often found together and appear to be tended by females. When handled it often writhes, musks, and pokes the handler with its harmless tail spine.

Rosy Boa *Lichanura trivirgata*

A medium-sized (to 950 mm or 37"), heavy-bodied snake with a blunt tail and three wide stripes on a cream or grayish tan background. Two forms, which might be separate species, occur in Arizona. The Mexican Rosy Boa has dark chocolate or black stripes and usually has scattered dark speckles on the pale belly. The Desert Rosy Boa has rusty orange to brown stripes and usually two distinct, parallel rows of blotches down the pale belly. Mexican Rosy Boas are found in Pima and southern Maricopa counties, whereas Desert Rosy Boas are found in west-central and extreme southwestern Arizona. Interestingly, this snake is unreported from the many mountains between the known  geographic ranges of the two forms. It is almost always found on or near rocky or boulder-strewn slopes in Sonoran Desertscrub, Mohave Desertscrub, or Interior Chaparral. Primarily nocturnal, but sometimes found crawling on mild mornings, early evening, and on overcast days. Most often encountered in spring. Preys on mammals and birds, perhaps relying heavily on nestlings. Capable of simultaneously constricting multiple prey. Mating probably occurs in the spring. An average of five young are born in late summer or fall.

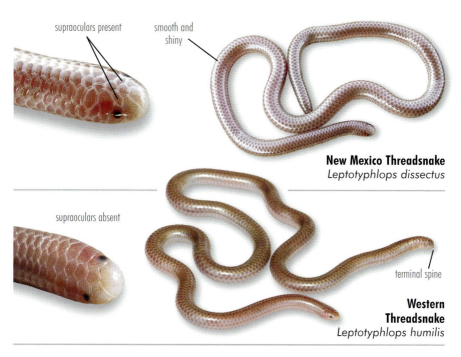

supraoculars present

smooth and shiny

New Mexico Threadsnake
Leptotyphlops dissectus

supraoculars absent

terminal spine

Western Threadsnake
Leptotyphlops humilis

Desert Rosy Boa

Rosy Boa
Lichanura trivirgata

Mexican Rosy Boa

vertical pupils

Sonoran Coralsnake *Micruroides euryxanthus*

VENOMOUS A small (to 615 mm or 24"), but long and uniformly slender snake. Red, black, and off-white (to yellow) bands encircle the body. Patches of black mottling are sometimes present in the red bands. A red marking usually covers the cloacal scute *(see p. 94)*. Found in communities ranging from Sonoran Desertscrub through Semidesert Grassland, into the lower edges of Madrean Evergreen Woodland and Great Basin Conifer Woodland. Primarily nocturnal, but sometimes found out on mild days. Although this docile snake rarely attempts to bite, its venom contains potent neurotoxins, and it should not be handled. Defensive behaviors include hiding the head within the coils, presenting the tail as a "false head", writhing, and forcefully everting the cloaca to produce a popping noise. Consumes small snakes, such as threadsnakes, groundsnakes, shovel-nosed snakes, black-headed snakes, and nightsnakes. Threadsnakes appear to be a preferred food. Lays 2–3 eggs during the monsoon season (July–August).

Sonoran Shovel-nosed Snake *Chionactis palarostris*

PROTECTED A small (to 430 mm or 17") yellow to cream snake with 20 or fewer black bands or saddles on the body. All but the forward-most (1–5) black bands completely encircle the body. Between the black bands are large, bright red saddles with indistinct margins. Flattened (slightly convex) snout, countersunk jaw, nasal valves, and concave belly are adaptations for life in loose sandy or gravelly soils. Usually found in or near washes on the middle bajada in Arizona Upland Desertscrub. In Arizona it is found exclusively on Organ Pipe Cactus National Monument where it is protected. Active March–October, most are found crossing roads on warm evenings in the spring. Eats a variety of invertebrates, including scorpions, centipedes, spiders, crickets and other insects. Probably mates in spring. Lays 4–5 eggs in early summer.

Western Shovel-nosed Snake *Chionactis occipitalis*

A small (to 369 mm or 15") pale yellow to cream snake with 21 or more black saddles or bands on the body. Three intergrading forms are found in Arizona: the Colorado Desert, Tucson, and Mohave Desert shovel-nosed snakes. In all three forms black bands encircle the posterior body and tail. The anterior black 'bands' do not completely cross the belly. Orange-red saddles between the black bands are sometimes flecked with black. In some forms, orange-red saddles are substantially reduced or absent. Flattened snout, countersunk jaw, nasal valves, and concave belly are adaptations for life in sandy environs. Often found in association with washes in Lower Colorado River Desertscrub and Mohave Desertscrub, but this snake appears to reach its highest densities in and around dunes. One form, the Tucson Shovel-nosed Snake, is apparently extirpated from much of its range including the Avra Valley. Primarily crepuscular, but can be found abroad throughout the night and in mild weather during the day. Eats a variety of invertebrates, including native roaches, scorpions, insect larvae, ants, solpugids, spiders, and reptile eggs. Where abundant this small snake is preyed upon by a variety of carnivores including various snakes, foxes, coyotes, shrikes, and owls. Males fight for access to receptive females. Mates in spring and lays 2–9 eggs in early summer.

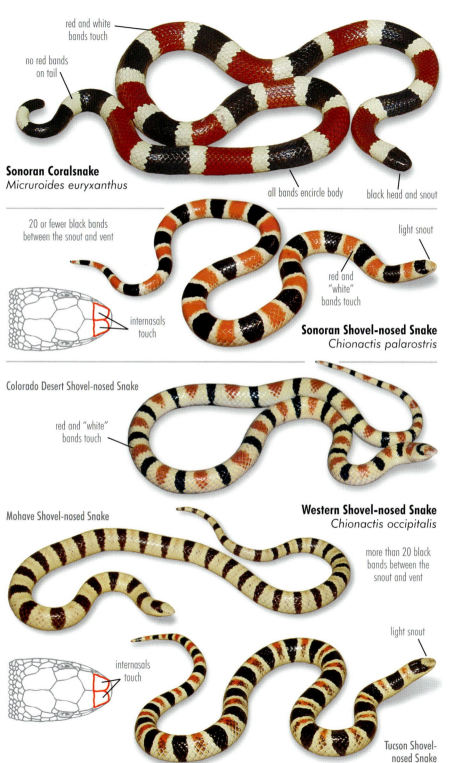

red and white
bands touch

no red bands
on tail

Sonoran Coralsnake
Micruroides euryxanthus

all bands encircle body

black head and snout

20 or fewer black bands
between the snout and vent

light snout

internasals
touch

red and
"white"
bands touch

Sonoran Shovel-nosed Snake
Chionactis palarostris

Colorado Desert Shovel-nosed Snake

red and "white"
bands touch

Mohave Shovel-nosed Snake

Western Shovel-nosed Snake
Chionactis occipitalis

more than 20 black
bands between the
snout and vent

light snout

internasals
touch

Tucson Shovel-
nosed Snake

Variable Sandsnake *Chilomeniscus stramineus*

A short (to 285 mm or 11"), stout snake with dark brown or black saddles on an orange and cream background. Tail is relatively short. Black markings form bands around the tail and saddles on the body. Belly is pale white to cream. Small eyes, nasal valves, an inset jaw, and a flattened, spade-like snout are adaptations for "swimming" through sand and burrowing through organic debris. In Arizona populations, the internasal scales do not touch each other, distinguishing this snake from shovel-nosed snakes and Groundsnakes. Primarily a denizen of Arizona Upland Desertscrub, but is also found along drainages above and below this community. Usually found in or near washes and other areas with fine to coarse sand and leaf litter. Crepuscular and nocturnal. Eats centipedes, native roaches, ants and their pupae, and other invertebrates. Preyed upon by ringtails, large scorpions, and other snakes. Probably mates in spring and lays 2–4 eggs in July and August. Hatchlings have been found in October.

Groundsnake *Sonora semiannulata*

A small (to 483 mm or 19") snake with highly variable pattern. Individuals can be banded, striped, or nearly unicolored. Background coloration can be tan, blue-gray, or light orange. Some have an orange mid-dorsal stripe, while others have black saddles or bands. Some otherwise unicolored Groundsnakes have a dark cap on the head and are easily confused with black-headed snakes. However, Groundsnakes have a loreal scale (*see p. 94*), whereas black-headed snakes do not. Groundsnakes also lack the reddish belly of our black-headed snakes. In the banded phase of the Groundsnake, red touches the black bands, whereas red and black are separated by white or cream in shovel-nosed snakes and the Sonoran Coral Snake. A small dark blotch at the base of each scale on the sides of Groundsnakes further distinguish them from black-headed snakes, shovel-nosed snakes, and Variable Sandsnakes. Groundsnakes occupy a wide variety of communities ranging from Lower Colorado River Desertscrub up into woodland, but appear to reach their highest densities in Arizona Upland Desertscrub and Semidesert Grassland. Although frequently found in back yards and vacant lots in Phoenix and Yuma, this snake appears to be absent from much of Tucson. Can be found out crawling both day and night. Eats various insects, as well as spiders, scorpions, centipedes, and occasionally small lizards. Mates in spring and lays 3–6 eggs in June or July. Hatchlings appear in July–August. Males will fight for access to receptive females.

Variable Sandsnake
Chilomeniscus stramineus

orange background

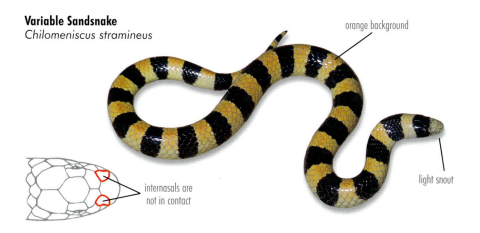

internasals are
not in contact

light snout

internasals
touch

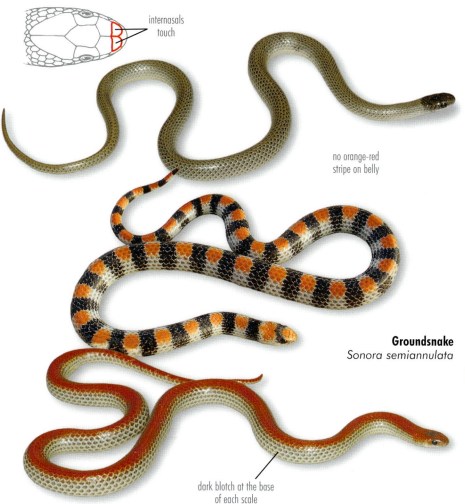

no orange-red
stripe on belly

Groundsnake
Sonora semiannulata

dark blotch at the base
of each scale

Plains Black-headed Snake *Tantilla nigriceps*

A small (to 380 mm or 15"), tan to yellowish brown snake with a black
or nearly black cap on the head. Light red or orange stripe down the
center of the belly. Black cap tapers to a point or is strongly convex
and extends three or more scales beyond the parietal furrow (*see p.
94*). Neck band absent. In Arizona, this snake is found in Semidesert
Grassland and Chihuahuan Desertscrub. Most often discovered
beneath surface objects, but sometimes found crossing roads on
humid evenings. Spring and monsoon rains bring them to the surface. Eats centipedes, millipedes, and scorpions, as well as adult and
larval insects. Lays 1–3 eggs that hatch in July or August.

Smith's Black-headed Snake *Tantilla hobartsmithi*

A small (to 313 mm or 12"), gray or tan snake with a black or nearly black cap on the head.
Light red or orange stripe down the center of the belly. Cap slightly convex or straight on rear
margin and extends only 1–3 scales behind the parietal furrow (*see p.
94*). Faint light collar sometimes visible along the trailing edge of the
black cap. Present in a wide variety of communities, including
Arizona Upland Desertscrub and Great Basin Conifer Woodland,
but is most abundant in Interior Chaparral and Semidesert Grassland. It can reach high densities in cottonwood-willow associations.
Spends most of its time underground or under rocks. Occasionally
found crossing roads at night. Eats centipedes, millipedes, scorpions,
and insect larvae. Reproductive biology poorly known, though an
Arizona specimen laid a single egg in August.

Yaqui Black-headed Snake *Tantilla yaquia*

A small (to 325 mm or 12.75"), tan to yellowish brown snake with a
black or nearly black cap on the head. White belly grading to pink or
orange posteriorly. The black cap extends well behind the parietal
furrow (*see p. 94*) and is bordered by a thin white collar. The cap
extends down the sides of the head to below the corner of the mouth,
contrasting with a prominent white cheek patch behind the eye. A
resident of Madrean Evergreen Woodland, it is usually found in
moist conditions under rocks or logs. In wet weather it has been collected while crossing paved roads. Probably eats a variety of small
invertebrates. Little is known of its reproductive biology.

Chihuahuan Black-headed Snake *Tantilla wilcoxi*

A small (to 350 mm or 14"), tan to yellowish brown snake with a dark brown head. Light red
or orange on the rear portion of the belly. Prominent, yellowish cream
neck band bordered by thin black lines crosses the posterior tips of the
parietals (*see p. 94*). Small, light cheek patch behind the eye. Belly
lacks black spotting, distinguishing this snake from the Ring-necked
Snake. In Arizona, this secretive snake is known from only three
small mountain ranges near the Mexican border. Occupies Madrean
Evergreen Woodland and Petran Montane Conifer Forest where it
spends most of its time underground. Often found beneath logs or
rocks in moist canyon bottoms. Probably eats invertebrates.
Reproductive biology undescribed.

cap pointed and extends 3 or more
scales beyond parietal furrow

Plains Black-headed Snake
Tantilla nigriceps

orange-red stripe on belly

cap slightly convex or straight
and extends less than 3 scales beyond parietal furrow

Smith's Black-headed Snake
Tantilla hobartsmithi

orange-red stripe on belly

cap extends
behind and
below corner
of mouth.

prominent
white cheek
patch

**Yaqui
Black-headed Snake**
Tantilla yaquia

pinkish-red on belly

orange-red belly

prominent collar
crosses rear edge
of the parietals

**Chihuahuan
Black-headed Snake**
Tantilla wilcoxi

Ring-necked Snake *Diadophis punctatus*

A small to medium, but long (to 857 mm or 34") and uniformly slender snake. Bluish gray to steel gray on the back. A pale orange or yellow ring often (but not always) marks the neck. Many specimens from western Arizona lack the neck ring. The underside grades from orangish yellow near the head to bright red below the tail, with small black spots throughout. Occupies a wide variety of upland biotic communities, from the desertscrubs to Petran Montane Conifer Forest. Most Arizona specimens have been collected from the edges of Madrean Evergreen Woodland. Usually encountered in the morning or near dusk. Defensive behaviors include writhing, musking, and exposing the bright underside of its tightly coiled tail. Feeds primarily on other snakes and lizards including gartersnakes, Groundsnakes, black-headed snakes, skinks, and the Madrean Alligator Lizard. Occasionally eats invertebrates. Enlarged rear teeth help deliver a venom that rapidly immobilizes some snakes and lizards, but does not appear to seriously affect mammals. Mates in spring and lays from 1–18 (average 5) eggs in June or July.

Nightsnake *Hypsiglena torquata*

A small (up to 598 mm or 23"), gray or tan snake with dark, brownish-gray blotches. The row of blotches on the back is usually single, although displacement along midline often gives the impression of two rows of offset blotches. A dark "collar" on the neck consists of one, two, or three blotches. Vertical pupils. Pale belly with no markings. Found in an extremely wide variety of habitats ranging from hot and dry Lower Colorado River Desertscrub through cool Petran Montane Conifer Forest. This crepuscular and nocturnal snake is regularly encountered by driving roads at night. Primarily consumes lizards, snakes and their eggs, but also frogs, toads, insects, and possibly scorpions. Its venom produces severe, often fatal hemorrhaging in snakes, but has minimal effect on mammals. Harmless to humans. Mates in spring. Lays an average of 3 or 4 eggs in June or July.

Western Lyresnake *Trimorphodon biscutatus*

A medium-sized (up to 1026 mm or 40"), gray snake with dark reddish brown, irregular, football-shaped blotches on the back. These blotches have hollow, pale gray centers and are outlined with pale gray lines. A prominent lyre-shaped marking adorns the top of the somewhat triangular head. The pupils are vertical. Primarily a species of our southern and western deserts. Well-documented populations in central Grand Canyon might be contiguous with populations to the southwest. Usually found in canyons, on rocky foothills, and on mountain slopes in Arizona Upland Desertscrub, Mohave Desertscrub, and Chihuahuan Desertscrub. Also found in Interior Chaparral, Madrean Evergreen Woodland, and Great Basin Conifer Woodland. Primarily nocturnal, though it can be found resting in rock fissures during the day. Lizards and bats are frequent prey, but rodents and birds are also taken. Although this species rapidly subdues lizards by envenomating them with grooved rear teeth, its venom does not appear to be much more than an irritant for humans. Also uses its coils to hold or constrict some prey. Mating season is undescribed. Lays 6–20 eggs which hatch in September or October.

collar sometimes absent

red underside
of tail

Ring-necked Snake
Diadophis punctatus

dark collar
(often broken)

vertical
pupil

Nightsnake
Hypsiglena torquata

irregular blotches with
light centers

Western Lyresnake
*Trimorphodon
biscutatus*

lyre-shaped
marking on head

vertical pupil

Gophersnake *Pituophis catenifer*

A large (to 2,337 mm or 92") and muscular snake. Grayish tan to creamy yellow with rusty brown dorsal blotches and smaller markings laterally. Mid-dorsal scales are keeled (*see p. 94*). The pale belly is usually marked with small dark blocks. One of our most common snakes. Found (at least occasionally) in every biotic community below Alpine Tundra, it is most abundant below about 1,980 m (~6,500'). Often abroad on mild days, but nocturnal during hot weather. Common in the diet of several raptors. Some hiss loudly, vibrate the tail, and strike when encountered and are consequently mistaken for rattlesnakes. Others are calm even when captured. This brawny constrictor feeds mostly on rodents, but also eats lizards, other snakes, and raids bird nests. Mates in spring, lays 2–24 eggs in June and July, and hatchlings start to appear in August.

Glossy Snake *Arizona elegans*

A medium-sized (to 1,055 mm or 42"), yellowish, gray, or faded tan snake with reddish brown blotches. The pale belly lacks markings. All dorsal scales are smooth (*see p. 94*) and shiny, distinguishing it from the Gophersnake, which has smooth scales on the sides and keeled scales mid-dorsally. A resident of desertscrub and grassland communities. Often found in open areas of shrubby desert with sandy or loamy soil. Primarily nocturnal, but sometimes found during the day. This constrictor consumes lizards, snakes, and small rodents. Mates in spring. Lays 2–24 eggs in late June or early July that hatch in August or September.

Spotted Leaf-nosed Snake *Phyllorhynchus decurtatus*

A small (to 510 mm or 20"), light tan or cream-colored snake with more than 17 small brown blotches on the body. Pale belly with no markings. Pupils elliptical. Found in Sonoran Desertscrub and Mohave Desertscrub, often on alluvial soils and bajadas. May occupy slightly rockier habitats than the Saddled Leaf-nosed Snake where the two species occur together. One of the more commonly encountered snakes at night during the hot, dry part of the summer, it is less frequently encountered at other times of the year. In the wild, this specialist feeds only on the eggs of lizards and snakes. The hard, protruding scale on the nose probably aids in excavating lizard nests. Lays 2–6 eggs in summer with hatching occurring from July to September.

Saddled Leaf-nosed Snake *Phyllorhynchus browni*

A small (to 508 mm or 20"), light tan or cream-colored snake with fewer than than 17 brown saddles on the body. Pale belly with no markings. Pupils elliptical. Found primarily in Arizona Upland Desertscrub in association with alluvial soils and bajadas, but sometimes found in Lower Colorado River Desertscrub flats. Active at night during the hot, dry part of the summer and less frequently encountered in other seasons. Commonly found crossing roads at night. This specialist feeds only on the eggs of lizards and snakes in the wild. The tough, protruding scale on the nose probably aids in excavating lizard nests. Lays 2–6 eggs in summer.

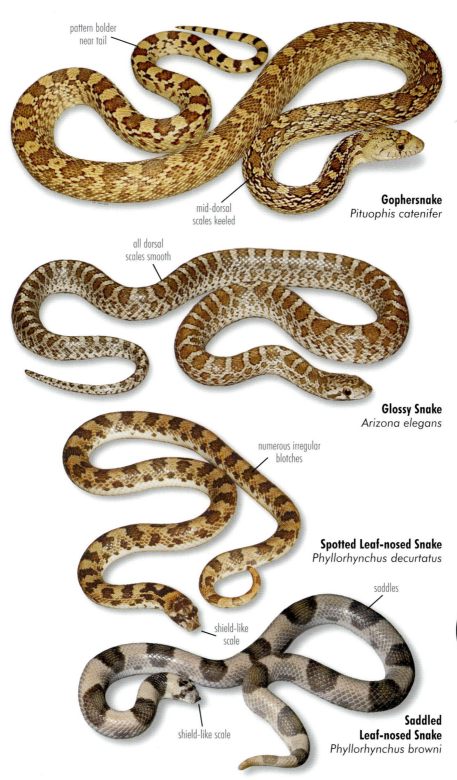

pattern bolder
near tail

mid-dorsal
scales keeled

Gophersnake
Pituophis catenifer

all dorsal
scales smooth

Glossy Snake
Arizona elegans

numerous irregular
blotches

Spotted Leaf-nosed Snake
Phyllorhynchus decurtatus

saddles

shield-like
scale

shield-like scale

**Saddled
Leaf-nosed Snake**
Phyllorhynchus browni

Western Hog-nosed Snake *Heterodon nasicus*

A small to medium-sized (to 760 mm or 30"), stout snake. Yellowish tan with darker brown blotches on the back and sides. The belly is black with yellowish tan block-shaped blotches. Prominent chocolate neck blotches and a chocolate "mask" adorn the head. Prominent sharply upturned snout. A Great Plains species, this snake is found exclusively in Semidesert Grassland and Chihuahuan Desertscrub in Arizona. Diurnal, though  seldom active mid-day, it is most often observed out and about on sunny mornings or late in the afternoon. When confronted by predators it often feigns death by flipping upside down, evacuating the cloaca, and gaping the mouth. Most abundant in areas with sandy or loamy soils, where it uses its snout to root out prey. Feeds on a wide variety of vertebrates, including toads, rodents, reptile eggs, lizards, snakes, and birds. Rear teeth deliver a venom that when chewed into humans can cause local swelling and discoloration. Mates in spring and lays 2–23 eggs in June or July. Hatchlings appear July–August.

Chihuahuan Hook-nosed Snake *Gyalopion canum*

A small (to 380 mm or 15"), gray to grayish tan snake. Brown blotches with zig-zag margins cross the back. The belly is creamy white and often suffused with salmon. Just behind the noticeably upturned snout is a slightly concave depression. Primarily  associated with Semidesert Grassland and Chihuahuan Desertscrub flatlands, but is sometimes found up in Madrean Evergreen Woodland. Little is known of the natural history of this infrequently encountered snake. It is most often encountered on roadways at night, usually during moist or humid conditions. Often writhes and forcefully everts the cloaca to produce a popping noise when handled. Eats spiders, scorpions, centipedes, and probably insects. May also feed on small lizards, snakes, and reptile eggs. The mating season is undescribed, though 1–4 eggs are laid in June or July.

Thornscrub Hook-nosed Snake *Gyalopion quadrangulare*

A small (to 300 mm or 12") but boldly and unusually patterned snake. Ground coloration consists of dark orangish-red sides and an off-white mid-dorsal stripe. Overlaying this is a series of black dorsal blotches, rectangular on the back and tapering to a point on the sides. These blotches are solid black dorsally, but become spotted with white on the sides. The belly is pale gray to cream. A black mask crosses the top of the head and eyes. Just  behind the noticeably upturned snout is a slightly concave depression. Primarily a denizen of thornscrub habitats in Mexico. In Arizona this snake is found in just a few borderland mountain ranges within Madrean Evergreen Woodland and hilly Mesquite-invaded Semidesert Grassland. In Arizona it is known only from specimens collected on roadways at night. Feeds on scorpions, spiders, insects and possibly centipedes, presumably by rooting through leaf litter and duff with its upturned snout. Mating season is undescribed. Lays up to six eggs.

Western Hog-nosed Snake
Heterodon nasicus

keeled scales

rostral
upturned
and keeled

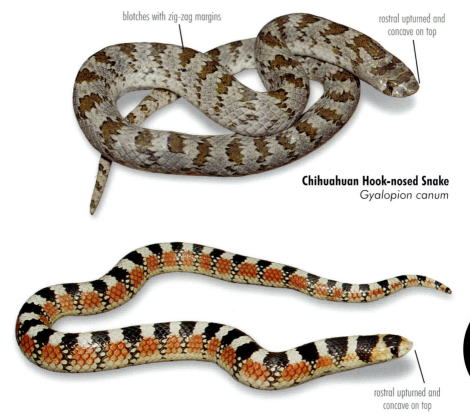

blotches with zig-zag margins

rostral upturned and
concave on top

Chihuahuan Hook-nosed Snake
Gyalopion canum

rostral upturned and
concave on top

Thornscrub Hook-nosed Snake
Gyalopion quadrangulare

Brown Vinesnake *Oxybelis aeneus*

A long (to 1,620 mm or 60") and exceptionally thin snake, aptly named for its resemblance to a vine. The head is long and narrow with a pointed snout and a dark line through the eye. Grayish brown to gray above, sometimes with dark linear flecking near midbody. The chin and throat are a bright creamy yellow that fades into a smooth, creamy gray, and immaculate belly. In Arizona, this predominantly tropical species is restricted to the Atascosa, Pajarito, and Patagonia mountains and adjacent mesquite basins along the Mexican border. Sightings and rumors of populations in the Baboquivari and Santa Rita mountains remain unconfirmed. Most often encountered on steep, grassy slopes in open Madrean Evergreen Woodland but also found in heavily wooded canyons. Highly arboreal. A visual predator, it relies on crypsis while stalking or ambushing prey. Lizards are its principal food, but frogs, fish, and insects are also taken. Grooved rear teeth help deliver a venom that rapidly immobilizes lizards, but is harmless to humans. Lays 3–8 eggs in summer and hatchlings appear in July and August.

Eastern Patch-nosed Snake *Salvadora grahamiae*

A medium-sized (to 900 mm or 35.5"), grayish tan to olive snake with two thick, dark brown or black stripes on its back. The space between these two stripes is yellowish cream to orangish tan. The sides are usually without stripes, but if side stripes are present they are thin and confined to the third scale row. Creamy yellow to white on the chin and throat, grading into a creamy white on the belly, to pinkish under the tail. Unlike the Western Patch-nosed Snake, the posterior chin scutes are either in contact or are separated by only one scale. This diurnal resident of Madrean Evergreen Woodland, Interior Chaparral, and Great Basin Conifer Woodland is usually found on open and rocky slopes. Feeds primarily on lizards and small snakes and their eggs, though small mammals and birds are also sometimes eaten. The large scale covering the snout protrudes slightly on the sides and is probably used to excavate reptile eggs. Probably mates in spring. Lays 3–10 eggs in summer and hatching occurrs in August or later.

Western Patch-nosed Snake *Salvadora hexalepis*

A medium-sized (1,014 mm or 40"), tan or peach snake with two thick, mottled stripes down the back. The space between these stripes is often peach or yellowish tan. Side stripes are thinner and are usually on the third and fourth scale rows. Pale cream belly sometimes suffused with pink or orange, especially near the tail. Unlike the Eastern Patch-nosed Snake, the posterior chin scutes are separated by two or more scales. Usually found on bajadas, rolling foothills, washes, and mountainsides from the desertscrubs into Great Basin Conifer Woodland and Madrean Evergreen Woodland. Its geographic range in northern Arizona is poorly known. This diurnal, fast, and alert snake feeds on reptile eggs, lizards, and small mammals. The large scale covering the snout protrudes slightly on the sides and is probably used to excavate reptile eggs. Mates in spring and lays 4–12 eggs in June and July. Hatchlings appear July through September.

Brown Vinesnake
Oxybelis aeneus

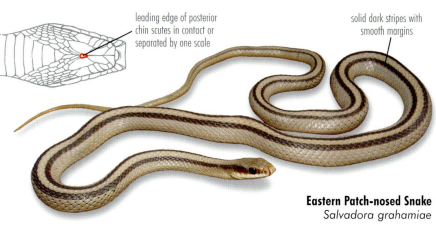

leading edge of posterior chin scutes in contact or separated by one scale

solid dark stripes with smooth margins

Eastern Patch-nosed Snake
Salvadora grahamiae

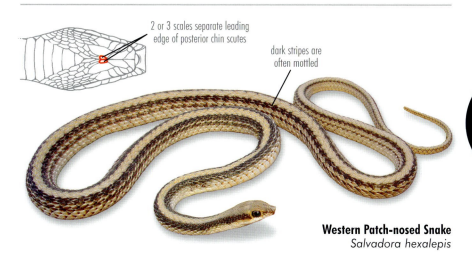

2 or 3 scales separate leading edge of posterior chin scutes

dark stripes are often mottled

Western Patch-nosed Snake
Salvadora hexalepis

Green Ratsnake *Senticolis triaspis*

A long (to 1,600 mm or 63"), plain green to yellowish green snake with an underside that grades from creamy white on the throat to yellowish beneath the tail. Hatchlings are gray and boldly patterned with a series of dark blotches down the back and smaller blotches on the sides. The juvenile pattern fades and becomes suffused with green as individuals age. Found in or adjacent to Madrean Evergreen Woodland on the rocky slopes of  our southeastern mountain ranges. Most specimens are encountered in ecotones between woodland and more open habitats or along riparian corridors. Despite persistent rumors, there are no vouchers supporting its presence in the Huachuca Mountains. Primarily terrestrial, it seeks refuge among rocks and under large boulders. Occasionally climbs trees or bushes in search of food. This crepuscular snake is seldom found late into the evening. Adults feed on rodents, bats, birds, and lizards. Juveniles might rely more heavily on lizards. Mates in spring and lays 2–9 eggs in June or July.

Sonoran Whipsnake *Masticophis bilineatus*

A long (up to 1,778 mm or 70"), bluish green or olive-brown snake that becomes increasingly lighter and more yellow toward mid-body and brownish-gray toward the rear. White flecking sometimes present throughout the dorsum. Two white or cream stripes on each side fade posteriorly. The belly is usually creamy white grading to yellowish under the tail. Can be discriminated from the Striped Whipsnake by pattern differences and the presence of 17 dorsal scale rows at midbody (*see p. 94*). Found in Arizona 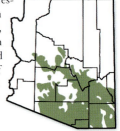 Upland Desertscrub foothills and mountains, Semidesert Grassland, Interior Chaparral, Madrean Evergreen Woodland, and Great Basin Conifer Woodland. Often found on sunny brushy slopes. Alert and fast-moving, it is a good climber and often retreats to the branches of bushes or trees when pursued. Like its cousins, the Coachwhip and Striped Whipsnake, it is an impressive predator that eats a broad variety of lizards, other snakes, rodents, bats, birds, and amphibians. Mating has been observed in June. Lays 6–13 eggs in June and July.

Striped Whipsnake *Masticophis taeniatus*

A long (up to 1,652 mm or 65"), dark brown to olive-brown snake with multiple white to cream stripes on the sides that are bisected by thin (often dashed) black lines. The underside is creamy yellow grading into coral pink or reddish under the tail. Dorsal scale rows (*see p. 94*) at midbody number 15, distinguishing it from the similar-looking Sonoran Whipsnake. Found in Semidesert Grassland, Interior Chaparral, Great Basin Conifer Woodland, and Plains and Great Basin Grassland. Less frequently found in Arizona  Upland Desertscrub and Petran Montane Conifer Forest. Distributed across much of northern Arizona in open brushy habitats and on rocky hills in grasslands. Seemingly disjunct populations occupy the Harcuvar, Harquahala, Kofa, Pinaleño, and Santa Teresa mountains. Diurnal, fast-moving, and alert, this lithe serpent is often heard moving through the brush before it is seen. Eats lizards, snakes, small mammals, birds, frogs, and insects. Mates in spring and lays 3–12 eggs in June and July, often in abandoned rodent burrows. Hatchlings appear in August and September.

juvenile

Green Ratsnake
Senticolis triaspis

adult

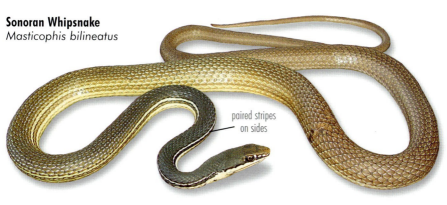

Sonoran Whipsnake
Masticophis bilineatus

paired stripes
on sides

Striped Whipsnake
Masticophis taeniatus

multiple stripes
on sides

Coachwhip *Masticophis flagellum*

A long (up to 1,728 mm or 68"), graceful serpent of variable color. Most are pinkish red, tan, or rust above. Some individuals are solid black above, while others are only black on part of the body. The underside is usually pinkish white grading to reddish under the tail. Abundant in Sonoran Desertscrub, Mohave Desertscrub, Chihuahuan Desertscrub, and Semidesert Grassland. Infrequently found in lower portions of Interior Chaparral. Abundant, conspicuous, and diurnal, this is one of the more commonly observed snakes in Arizona, though often fleetingly. When frightened it flees so rapidly that it seems to magically disappear into the desert. Although seldom captured, it rapidly and repeatedly bites when handled. Sometimes feigns death when persistently harassed. Fast and exceptionally alert, this is arguably the most extraordinary and behaviorally versatile predator in the Sonoran Desert. It actively hunts during the day for lizards and other snakes (including rattlesnakes), raids bird nests, and lies in ambush outside mine shafts waiting for emerging bats, which are snatched from the air. Rodents, frogs, toads, small turtles, insects, and carrion are also taken. Mates in spring and lays 4–24 eggs in June and July. Hatchlings appear in August and September.

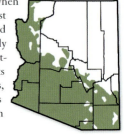

Eastern Racer *Coluber constrictor*

A long (to 1,900 mm or 75"), bluish green to olive snake with a creamy lemon-yellow belly. Juveniles are strongly patterned with brown or reddish brown blotches on a light olive-gray to tan background. Smaller blotching of similar coloration is present on the sides. This pattern fades with age and is gradually replaced by the greenish pattern of adult snakes. A surprisingly versatile snake that has been found in all 48 continental states. It occupies an amazing variety of habitats across its range. In general it is associated with moist, open grassy situations or ecotones between forest and grassland. Despite its abundance in many places throughout its broad range, this is Arizona's rarest snake. It is documented in our state by a single specimen collected from "Eagar, Arizona" in 1927. Although 80 years have elapsed, it may yet be found along the banks of the Little Colorado River, or further south among the woodland and forest communities that surround its headwaters. Here, other primarily eastern species, such as Thirteen-lined Ground Squirrels, make their only appearance within Arizona. This diurnal and versatile predator feeds on a tremendous variety of reptiles, amphibians, small mammals, and invertebrates. Mates in spring and lays an average of 14 eggs in summer.

black phase

red phase

Coachwhip
Masticophis flagellum

adult

juvenile

Eastern Racer
Coluber constrictor

Long-nosed Snake *Rhinocheilus lecontei*

A medium-sized (to 892 mm or 35"), lean snake with a highly variable pattern. Black saddles on the back are ringed by a thin white line and are often marked with white speckles on the sides of the body. Spaces between the saddles are white, yellowish cream, pink, or red and are often flecked with black. Some appear virtually black and white banded. Many have patterns intermediate between those pictured here. The belly is typically cream with some speckling. Found in a broad variety of communities, including Sonoran Desertscrub, Chihuahuan Desertscrub, Mohave Desertscrub, Interior Chaparral, Great Basin Conifer Woodland, and Plains and Great Basin Grassland. Primarily crepuscular and nocturnal. When handled it often writhes and sometimes everts the cloaca, releasing blood and foul-smelling waste to repel would-be predators. Whiptail lizards (*Aspidoscelis*) comprise about half of this constrictor's diet, but it also eats a variety of other lizards, lizard eggs, snake eggs, and small mammals. Probably mates in spring. Lays 3–11 eggs in June, July, or August. Hatchlings appear in late August.

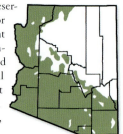

Common Kingsnake *Lampropeltis getula*

A large (to 1,422 mm or 56"), variably patterned snake. Three forms occur in Arizona: the California Kingsnake, Desert Kingsnake, and Western Black Kingsnake. The California Kingsnake is black with narrow white or yellowish bands that widen on the lower sides. The Desert Kingsnake is black, but speckled with yellow in a pattern that creates a series of dark black blotches down the center of the back. The Western Black Kingsnake is completely black or nearly so. Solid black kingsnakes have been found in south-central Arizona from the vicinity of Tucson south to Nogales. Black specimens have also been found near Douglas, and at other points along the Mexican border. The Desert Kingsnake is known from Santa Cruz County, much of Cochise County, and extreme eastern Pima County. The California Kingsnake occurs in much of the rest of the state. Intergrades are found along contact zones in southeastern Arizona. Occupies Sonoran Desertscrub, Chihuahuan Desertscrub, Mohave Desertscrub, Great Basin Desertscrub, Semidesert Grassland, and Plains and Great Basin Grassland. Occasionally found in Interior Chaparral, Great Basin Conifer Woodland, and Madrean Evergreen Woodland. Primarily nocturnal, but occasionally abroad on overcast or mild days. Of variable disposition, this snake will sometimes exude musk when handled. A powerful constrictor with a broad diet consisting of snakes (including rattlesnakes), lizards, small mammals, nestling and adult birds, and perhaps frogs and toads. Mates in spring and lays 2–24 eggs in late June or July. Hatchlings begin to appear in late August.

Long-nosed Snake
Rhinocheilus lecontei

black saddles do
not cross belly

light flecking in
dark bands

California
Kingsnake

Common Kingsnake
Lampropeltis getula

white bands
widen toward
belly

Western Black
Kingsnake

Desert
Kingsnake

Sonoran Mountain Kingsnake *Lampropeltis pyromelana*

A medium-sized (to 1,088 mm or 43") snake with alternating red, black, and white bands. The black bands occur between the red and white bands. Black bands often widen into the red bands mid-dorsally, sometimes connecting and pinching the red bands in half. The snout is white or creamy gray, sometimes with black mottling. Found primarily in mountainous terrain within Interior Chaparral, Great Basin Conifer Woodland, Madrean Evergreen Woodland, and Petran Montane Conifer Forest. Known from most of the Mogollon Rim country and many of the Sky Islands. It has not yet been vouchered in the Cerbat, Dragoon, Galiuro, Santa Teresa, or Winchester mountains. In addition, it is curiously undocumented from the forested south rim of the Grand Canyon where the habitat seems appropriate. Most often found in rocky areas with abundant leaf litter and canopy cover. Steep wooded canyons are a favored place to search for this animal. Primarily diurnal, but occasionally found crawling at night. This colorful snake often writhes, bites, and exudes musk in response to handling. Proficient at climbing trees and raiding bird nests. A strong constrictor, it consumes lizards, rodents, birds, and rarely bats. Clutches of 2–9 eggs are laid in June and early July, and hatchlings appear in July and August.

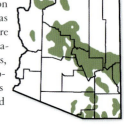

Milksnake *Lampropeltis triangulum*

PROTECTED throughout Cochise County. A medium-sized (to 900 mm or 35.5") snake banded in black, red, and yellowish white. Black bands occur between the red and yellowish white bands. Black bands sometimes broaden mid-dorsally, occasionally connecting with one another and thus bisecting the intervening red band. Head and snout are black, sometimes with red or white flecks. A white band crosses the back of the head and top of the neck. Though infrequently encountered in Arizona, this secretive and fossorial snake is broadly distributed across the northern part of the state in Plains and Great Basin Grassland. Locally abundant in some areas, it nevertheless can be difficult to find. Though suitable habitat exists on the Coconino Plateau and on the Arizona Strip, Milksnakes have not yet been vouchered from these expansive landscapes. In southern Arizona, another form of this species was recently discovered. This apparently isolated population appears to be restricted to a patch of relict grassland. A secretive species, Milksnakes might yet be documented further west in the grassland valleys of Cochise and Santa Cruz counties. Eats a wide variety of reptiles and small mammals and occasionally birds, amphibians, and insects. Mates in spring and lays 1–24 eggs in late spring or summer.

white snout

red touches
black

Sonoran Mountain Kingsnake
Lampropeltis pyromelana

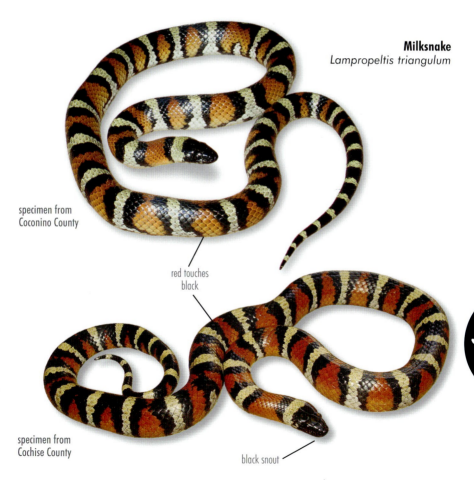

Milksnake
Lampropeltis triangulum

specimen from
Coconino County

red touches
black

specimen from
Cochise County

black snout

Black-necked Gartersnake *Thamnophis cyrtopsis*

A medium-sized (up to 1,070 mm or 42"), dark gray to olive-gray snake with an orange-yellow mid-dorsal stripe and a light cream side stripe on the second and third scale rows. Black spots between the stripes. Bluish gray head with two conspicuous, crescent-shaped black blotches on the neck. Light gray and unmarked belly. Found in upper portions of Arizona Upland Desertscrub, through Interior Chaparral, Great Basin Conifer Woodland, Madrean Evergreen Woodland, into lower Petran Montane Conifer Forest. 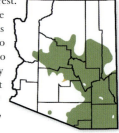 Principally an upland species, it is essentially distributed along the Mogollon Rim and Sky Islands. Isolated populations follow creeks and canyons that flow north from the Rim across the Colorado Plateau. A disjunct and isolated population is also present in the Ajo Mountains and adjacent Tohono O'odham reservation. Usually found near water in rocky canyons or semi-permanent streams, but occasionally found far from water. Active day and night, especially during moist or mild weather. Eats frogs, toads, tadpoles, lizards, and invertebrates. Young are born in late June and July.

Terrestrial Gartersnake *Thamnophis elegans*

A medium-sized (up to 900 mm or 35.5"), reddish brown, brownish olive, or gray snake with a single cream mid-dorsal stripe. Black spots appear on the back and sides and often infringe upon the mid-dorsal stripe. Some individuals lack stripes. If present, the side stripe is on the second and third scale rows on the anterior part of the body. Dark marks on the neck are usually diffuse and are sometimes absent. Pale below. Occupies Great Basin  Conifer Woodland, Petran Montane Conifer Forest, Petran Subalpine Conifer Forest, Great Basin Desertscrub, and Plains and Great Basin Grassland. In Arizona, it is found across much of the Colorado Plateau and at the highest elevations in Mogollon Rim country. Isolated populations occupy the Sierra Ancha and Pinaleño mountains. A diurnal predator and true generalist, this snake forages on a wide variety of prey, including rodents, birds, lizards, bats, salamanders, rabbits, frogs, toads, fish, insects, and worms. Mates in spring and gives birth to 3–27 (average of 8) young in July and August.

Checkered Gartersnake *Thamnophis marcianus*

A medium-sized (up to 1,088 mm or 43"), olive-green snake with a pale stripe down the middle of the back. Light cream side stripes are restricted to the third scale row. Black spots appear in a checkerboard pattern between the stripes. Spots often infringe upon the mid-dorsal stripe. Olive-green head with two conspicuous, dark olive-gray or brownish neck blotches that are boldly edged in black. Light creamy gray below. Occupies Semidesert  Grassland, Chihuahuan Desertscrub, and Lower Colorado River Desertscrub. This species is significantly expanding its range in association with the proliferation of agriculture, cattle tanks, and other water developments. There are isolated records from the lower Colorado River in the vicinity of Yuma. Seems to prefer the vicinity of ponds, tanks, and river basins, but during rainy or humid weather it can be found far from standing water. Active day and night. Eats frogs, toads, fish, lizards, invertebrates, and probably small mammals. Young are born late June through July.

bright orange-yellow mid-dorsal stripe

side stripe on scale rows 2 and 3

jet black neck crescents

Counting scale rows:

4   3   2   1   belly scale

Black-necked Gartersnake
Thamnophis cyrtopsis

neck blotches diffuse or absent

spots often infringe on mid-dorsal stripe

Terrestrial Gartersnake
Thamnophis elegans

side stripe on scale rows 2 and 3

spots often infringe on dorsal stripe

side stripe on 3rd scale row

Checkered Gartersnake
Thamnophis marcianus

black margins on neck blotches

Mexican Gartersnake *Thamnophis eques*

PROTECTED A medium-sized (up to 1,120 mm or 44"), rust or olive-brown snake with a creamy yellow mid-dorsal stripe. Margins of the mid-dorsal stripe are often delineated by thin black lines. On the anterior part of the body the side stripe is on the third and fourth scale rows. Little groups of small black dash marks form blotches between the stripes. If present, dark neck blotches are diffuse. Pale below. Found in communities ranging from Sonoran Desert-scrub through Semidesert Grassland, Interior Chaparral, Madrean Evergreen Woodland, into lower reaches of Petran Montane Conifer Forest. A species of streams, rivers, ciénegas, and ponds with thick bank vegetation. Museum vouchers suggest this species was once broadly distributed in southern Arizona along perennial stretches of the Colo-rado and Gila river systems. It now appears to be extirpated from the Agua Fria, Colorado, Gila, Salt, and most of the Santa Cruz and San Pedro rivers. Also appears to be extirpated from the Tucson Basin. Populations remain in only a handful of streams draining the Mogol-lon Rim and a few streams and ciénegas in southeastern Arizona. Status of populations on the White Mountain Apache Reservation and near Lakeside are unknown. This diurnal predator actively for-ages for frogs, toads, tadpoles, fish, invertebrates, and sometimes lizards and small mammals. Young are born June through early July.

Narrow-headed Gartersnake *Thamnophis rufipunctatus*

PROTECTED A medium-sized (up to 1,115 mm or 44"), olive, reddish brown, or charcoal-colored snake with paired dark reddish brown to gray blotches on the back. The underside is pale creamy yellow grading into grayish brown posteriorly. A double row of dark markings is often present on the belly. Its common name alludes to its long, narrow snout. This extreme-ly aquatic snake is found in rocky, perennial streams and rivers in communities ranging from Petran Montane Conifer Forest, through Great Basin Conifer Woodland and Interior Chapar-ral, into upper portions of Arizona Upland Desertscrub. Populations in Arizona and New Mexico are disappearing at an alarming rate, probably in response to the introduction of non-native predators such as crayfish, bass, and catfish. Where crayfish have invaded, Narrow-headed Gartersnakes often have scars on their bodies, are missing their tails, or both. Over-grazing may negatively affect populations by eroding banks, denuding streamside vegetation (important basking sites), and increasing sedimentation (covering rocky foraging sites). Water diversions, heavy recreational use, and stream sterilization or heavy sed-imentations following wildfires may have negatively affected popula-tions in some streams. In most of our rivers and streams this garter-snake has either been completely extirpated, reduced in number, or is restricted to short stretches. Seldom wanders far from streams and riparian habitat during the summer. Hibernates in rocky ledges high above the floodline. Diurnal, it basks in willows or other vegetation overhanging rocky, clear streams. Primarily an ambush predator, it forages underwater for native suckers, dace, chub, and small trout. Mates in spring and gives birth to 8–18 young in July or August.

Mexican Gartersnake
Thamnophis eques

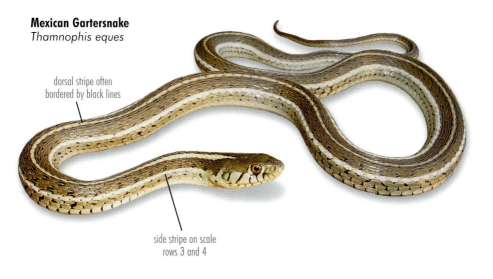

dorsal stripe often
bordered by black lines

side stripe on scale
rows 3 and 4

Narrow-headed Gartersnake
Thamnophis rufipunctatus

no dorsal stripe

Western Diamond-backed Rattlesnake *Crotalus atrox*

VENOMOUS Arizona's largest rattlesnake (up to 1,676 mm or 66"). Gray to tan with "salt and pepper" flecking throughout and brown diamond-shaped blotches on the back. Black and white bands on the tail are usually roughly equal in width. Posterior light eye stripe crosses the lip forward of the corner of the mouth. Sometimes three, but usually four or more scales separate the supraoculars anteriorly *(see facing page)*. Found from Lower Colorado River Desert-scrub up into Great Basin Conifer Woodland and Madrean Evergreen Woodland, but most abundant in Arizona Upland Desertscrub and Chihuahuan Desertscrub. Seldom found far from rocky ground or bajadas. Predominantly nocturnal but also active on mild days. Pack rat nests are a favorite refuge during the day. Hibernates alone or in groups in rock outcrops, crevices, or Wood Rat nests. Chiefly an ambush predator, it lies in wait for small mammals (including rabbits), birds, or lizards. Large venom yields and potent hemorrhagic toxins can result in severe tissue damage. Mates in spring and again during the monsoon. Gives birth to 2–12 young just before the monsoon.

Mohave Rattlesnake *Crotalus scutulatus*

VENOMOUS A large rattlesnake (up to 1,270 mm or 50"). Green, gray, or tan with a series of dark brown diamond shaped or roughly rectangular blotches (usually ringed in black and then again in light cream). "Salt and pepper" flecking absent. Black bands are usually narrower than white bands on the tail. Rarely, the tail bands are reduced or consist of alternating light and dark brown bands (resulting in a tail that resembles that of the Western Rattlesnake or Prairie Rattlesnake). Posterior light eye stripe extends back beyond the corner of the mouth and does not cross the lip. Two scales separate the supraocular scales anteriorly*(see facing page)*. Most abundant in Semidesert Grassland, Sonoran Desertscrub, Mohave Desertscrub, and Chihuahuan Desertscrub. Open grasslands often support high densities of this primarily nocturnal snake. Feeds mostly on small mammals, but also eats birds, lizards, frogs, and toads. Younger snakes feed more heavily on lizards. Venom composition varies throughout Arizona; potent neurotoxins (particularly in southeastern Arizona) and large venom yields make this species very dangerous. Mates in spring and again during the monsoon. Gives birth to 2–17 young during the monsoon.

Black-tailed Rattlesnake *Crotalus molossus*

VENOMOUS A large (up to 1,219 mm or 48"), olive-brown to yellow-brown rattlesnake. Conspicuous dark blotches on the back have a few light scales within their margins. Black tail, sometimes faintly banded. The top of the snout is often gray or black. This remarkably versatile generalist occurs in habitats ranging from isolated boulder piles in Lower Colorado River Desertscrub up into exposed southern rock slides in Petran Subalpine Conifer Forest. Most abundant in Interior Chaparral, Great Basin Conifer Woodland, Madrean Evergreen Woodland, and Petran Montane Conifer Forest. Almost always associated with rocky or mountainous terrain. Primarily a crepuscular and nocturnal hunter, but often found sheltered beneath vegetation during the day. In mild weather, it can be found out crawling at all hours. Eats small mammals, including rabbits, and perhaps infrequently consumes other reptiles. Its especially large venom yields and potent hemorrhagic toxins can produce severe tissue damage and necrosis. Mating takes place July through September, and 3–16 young are born during the monsoon season.

Western Diamond-backed Rattlesnake
Crotalus atrox

black and white bands **roughly** equal in width

light eye stripe crosses lip

3 or more scales separate supraoculars anteriorly

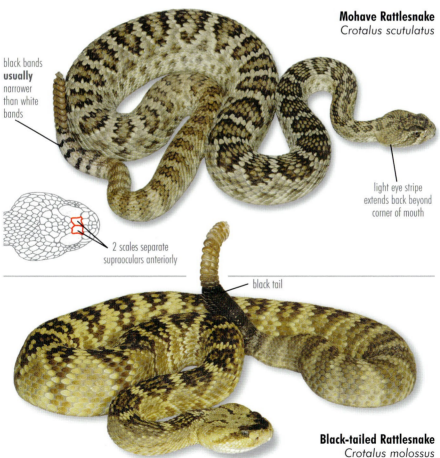

Mohave Rattlesnake
Crotalus scutulatus

black bands **usually** narrower than white bands

light eye stripe extends back beyond corner of mouth

2 scales separate supraoculars anteriorly

black tail

Black-tailed Rattlesnake
Crotalus molossus

Sidewinder *Crotalus cerastes*

VENOMOUS A small (up to 628 mm or 25"), tan rattlesnake with darker brown blotches. The spaces between the blotches are white. Scales above the eyes are raised and horn-like. Thin black bands mark the end of the tail. Strongly associated with Lower Colorado River Desertscrub and Mohave Desertscrub. Almost always found in relatively flat, open desert with sandy or loamy soil. Most abundant in and around dunes and in Creosotebush flats. Primarily nocturnal but can be found on the surface during the day, often cratered into the sand near the base of a shady bush. Its unique method of moving across sandy soil (side-winding) leaves easily identifiable J-shaped tracks. Feeds primarily on lizards and small mammals, but also takes birds and snakes. Low venom yields and relatively low toxicity. Unlike most other rattlesnakes, male fighting has not been documented in Sidewinders. Mates in spring and possibly again in fall. Gives birth to 1-20 young during the monsoon season.

Tiger Rattlesnake *Crotalus tigris*

VENOMOUS A medium-sized (up to 885 mm or 35"), blue-gray to orange-red rattlesnake. Peach or orange suffusion is often present on the lower sides. Dark and sometimes diffuse "tiger" bands cross the back. Often confused with the Speckled Rattlesnake, the Tiger Rattlesnake usually lacks black bands near the tip of the tail, has a much smaller head relative to the body size, and the rostral scale touches the nasal scales (*see p. 94*). Principally a creature of Arizona Upland Desertscrub foothills and mountains but also found in Interior Chaparral and Madrean Evergreen Woodland. Occasionally found in Lower Colorado River Desertscrub, but usually within a mile of rocky habitat or foothills. A population was recently discovered within Chihuahuan Desertscrub in the southern Peloncillo Mountains. Primarily nocturnal, but sometimes abroad on mild days. Eats small mammals and lizards. Low venom yields, but potent neurotoxins render the venom exceptionally toxic, perhaps the most toxic of the rattlesnakes. Mates and gives birth to 2–6 young during the monsoon.

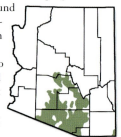

Speckled Rattlesnake *Crotalus mitchellii*

VENOMOUS A large (up to 1,295 mm or 51"), bluish gray, grayish white, peach, or reddish rattlesnake. Highly variable background coloration sometimes matches the soil or rocks of its habitat. Speckling on the back forms diffuse blotches that resemble bands toward the tail. Sometimes prominently banded. In Arizona, a row of small scales separates the rostral from each prenasal, distinguishing the Speckled Rattlesnake from other Arizona rattlesnakes (*see facing page*). Black bands usually present near the tip of the tail. Found in Sonoran and Mohave Desertscrub communities, sometimes ranging up into Interior Chaparral. Often found in exceptionally rocky canyons and on rock and boulder strewn slopes. Old mines, seeps, and springs seem to be favored haunts. Primarily nocturnal, but also active on mild days. Abundant along the Colorado River in the lower Grand Canyon where it occurs as far upstream as Havasu Canyon. Here, it is often confused with the Grand Canyon Rattlesnake due to a shared pinkish hue and faded pattern. Eats small mammals, birds, and lizards. Moderate venom yields with potent hemorrhagic toxins. Mates in spring. Young are born mainly from July through August.

dark bands near tail tip

horn-like
supraoculars

Sidewinder
Crotalus cerastes

white between dorsal blotches

Tiger Rattlesnake
Crotalus tigris

disproportionately
small head

row of small scales separates
rostral from prenasals

Speckled Rattlesnake
Crotalus mitchellii

black bands near tail tip

127

Arizona Black Rattlesnake *Crotalus cerberus*

VENOMOUS A large (up to 1,062 mm or 42"), dark brown, dark gray, to nearly solid black rattlesnake with black blotches down the back. Spaces between the blotches often form yellowish or white crossbars. Young are light gray or tan with prominent facial markings and dark blotches. Young darken gradually as they age. Four or more internasals contact the rostral *(see facing page)*, distinguishing it from Mohave and Black-tailed rattlesnakes which usually have three or fewer internasals contacting the rostral. Nearly endemic to Arizona, this snake can be found outside our state only in extreme west-central New Mexico. Sometimes erroneously referred to as Timber Rattlesnakes (*Crotalus horridus*), which are native to the eastern United States and do not occur in Arizona. The Arizona Black Rattlesnake is primarily a denizen of Interior Chaparral, Great Basin Conifer Woodland, Madrean Evergreen Woodland, and Petran Montane Conifer Forest, but is sometimes found high in Arizona Upland Desertscrub. Often encountered in canyon bottoms, on dry rocky slopes, and in rock slides. Active day or night, when conditions are favorable. Eats small mammals, lizards, and birds. Moderate venom yields with potent hemorrhagic toxins. Young are born during July and August.

Western Rattlesnake *Crotalus oreganus*

VENOMOUS A generally large (up to 1,650 mm or 63") snake with highly variable background coloration and large dorsal blotches. Four or more internasals contact the rostral *(see facing page)*, distinguishing this snake from the Mohave Rattlesnake which usually has three or fewer internasals contacting the rostral. Three forms occur in Arizona. The Great Basin Rattlesnake tends toward gray or straw yellow, with suffusions of pink or salmon. Prominent blotches on the back usually take the form of black rings filled with darker background color. The Grand Canyon Rattlesnake ranges from grayish tan to pinkish or salmon with faded tan or reddish gray blotches on the back. Exceptionally old individuals sometimes lack pattern altogether. The Midget Faded Rattlesnake is generally straw, pale gray, or sandy tan colored and is the smallest of the three forms found in Arizona. The centers of the body blotches tend to be the same color as the background, perhaps a slightly darker hue, with a thin dark-edged margin. Western Rattlesnakes occupy Mohave Desertscrub, Great Basin Desertscrub, Plains and Great Basin Grassland, and Great Basin Conifer Woodland. Great Basin Rattlesnakes are found on the high plains and plateaus north and west of the Colorado River. Grand Canyon Rattlesnakes are found exclusively within Grand Canyon or within a few miles of its rim, from Powell Reservoir downstream to the vicinity of Tuckup Canyon. In Arizona, the Midget Faded Rattlesnake has only been found in a few small canyons in the general vicinity of Powell Reservoir. There appears to be considerable genetic exchange between the three forms of this species (*C. oreganus*) where they meet along the rims and side canyons of Grand Canyon. Snakes that appear to be hybrids between the Western Rattlesnake and Prairie Rattlesnake can be found in the vicinity of the Echo Cliffs. Primarily nocturnal, though often active during the day in the spring and fall. In and around Grand Canyon, this snake is most often encountered near water. Rodents, birds, and the occasional lizard are the regular fare of this serpent. Venom composition is variable, but is generally moderately toxic. Midget Faded Rattlesnake and some Grand Canyon Rattlesnake venoms are very toxic, and contain neurotoxins. Young are born in July and August.

light bars between blotches

adult

juvenile

Arizona Black Rattlesnake
Crotalus cerberus

Great Basin Rattlesnake

Western Rattlesnake
Crotalus oreganus

Grand Canyon Rattlesnake

four or more internasals touch the rostral

Midget Faded Rattlesnake

Prairie Rattlesnake *Crotalus viridis*

VENOMOUS A generally large (up to 1,620 mm or 64") rattlesnake represented by two forms in Arizona. The larger Green Prairie Rattlesnake is sometimes greenish, but more often is tan with brown dorsal blotches and smaller blotches on the sides. The smaller Hopi Rattlesnake usually does not grow longer than 700 mm or 27.5" and is typically tan or sandy brown with chocolate blotches. In both forms four or more internasal scales contact the rostral (*see facing page*) distinguishing them from the Mohave Rattlesnake, which has 3 or fewer internasals contacting the rostral. A thin white line often forms the margin of the blotches. Green Prairie Rattlesnakes have only been documented in Arizona in the general vicinity of Springerville. Despite persistent rumors, a specimen has not yet been produced from Cochise County, although the species has been found tantalizingly close to the border at Antelope Pass, Hidalgo County, New Mexico. Hopi Rattlesnakes can be found across much of the Colorado Plateau in Plains and Great Basin Grassland and Great Basin Desertscrub. Hybridizes with

the Western Rattlesnake in the vicinity of Echo Cliffs. As its common name suggests, this snake is adapted for wide open grasslands, and its overall range maps almost exactly onto the Great Plains. On largely rockless plains, this snake uses rodent burrows as temporary refuges and hibernacula. Green Prairie Rattlesnakes will hibernate in large groups (100's) in prairie dog towns or rocky refuges, though communal hibernation is undescribed in Hopi Rattlesnakes. Primarily nocturnal, but crepuscular during cooler seasons. Diet consists mostly of small mammals and birds, but lizards are also taken. Moderately toxic venom. Mates and gives birth in July and August.

Massasauga *Sistrurus catenatus*

VENOMOUS • **PROTECTED** A small (up to 550 mm or 22") rattlesnake with a narrow head and a small rattle. Coloration is pale gray to silverish near the spine, becoming suffused with rust on the sides. Dorsal blotches are elliptical, dark chocolate, and outlined with a smooth, thin black line. Additional rows of blotches are present on the sides. Two blotches on the head extend back onto the neck, forming a lyre-shape. Tail is yellow at birth, but within a year changes to the adult form of light gray with brown bands. Unlike other Arizona rattlesnakes which have numerous small scales on the top of the head, the scales on the top of the Massasauga's head are large and plate-like (*see facing page*). In Arizona this snake is found exclusively in Semidesert Grassland. Populations in the northern San Simon Valley (east of Safford), the Suphur Springs Valley, and southern San Pedro Valley appear to be extirpated, perhaps due to degradation of grassland habitat or development. Arizona's sole surviv-

ing population is found in Tobosa grassland on the divide between the San Simon and San Bernardino valleys. Primarily nocturnal, though sometimes found coiled at the base of bunchgrass during the day. Hibernates and shelters in rodent burrows. Preys mostly on lizards and giant centipedes, but also takes a variety of small mammals. Young snakes lure lizards to within striking distance by slowly wriggling their brightly colored tails. Venom is highly toxic, but yields are low. Arizona specimens give birth to 4–8 young in August or September.

four or more internasals
touch the rostral

Green Prairie Rattlesnake

Prairie Rattlesnake
Crotalus viridis

Hopi Rattlesnake

large plate-like scales on top of head

Massasauga
Sistrurus catenatus

Twin-spotted Rattlesnake *Crotalus pricei*

VENOMOUS • **PROTECTED** A small (up to 660 mm or 26") gray to reddish brown rattlesnake with paired dark brown or dark gray dorsal blotches. The proximal rattle segment (*see page 94*) is orange. Young snakes have orangish tail tips which they may use to lure lizards. In Arizona, it is known only from the Chiricahua, Huachuca, Pinaleño, and Santa Rita mountains. It occupies Petran Montane Conifer Forest and Petran Subalpine Conifer Forest communities; occasionally found as low as Madrean Evergreen Woodland. Although most often found within or near large rock slides, it also inhabits adjacent forest and canyon bottoms. Primarily diurnal. Feeds most often on lizards, but will also take small mammals and birds. Venom may be highly toxic, but yields are low. Mates in July and August and gives birth to 3–9 young in July and August.

Rock Rattlesnake *Crotalus lepidus*

VENOMOUS • **PROTECTED** A small (up to 840 mm or 33") gray to greenish gray rattlesnake with black bands over the back. Black speckling and mottling between the black bands in most Arizona specimens. Juveniles have bright orange tails that fade somewhat as they age. Males tend to be greener than females, especially mid-dorsally. In Arizona, this small mountain rattlesnake is restricted to Madrean Evergreen Woodland and Petran Montane Conifer Forest. Rock slides and open, rocky slopes appear to be preferred habitats within these communities, but this rattlesnake can also be found along wooded canyon bottoms. Found throughout most of the sky islands, but curiously absent from the Mule and Patagonia Mountains. Its range in New Mexico suggests that it may yet be discovered in east-central Greenlee County. Preys mainly on giant centipedes and lizards, but small mammals and rarely small birds are also taken. Juveniles lure lizards to within striking distance by slowly wriggling their brightly colored tails. Toxic venom, but yields are low. Mates from July–September. Gives birth to 1–10 young in July or August.

Ridge-nosed Rattlesnake *Crotalus willardi*

VENOMOUS • **PROTECTED** A small (up to 668 mm or 26"), graceful rattlesnake represented by two forms in Arizona. The Arizona Ridge-nosed Rattlesnake (our state reptile) is orange-brown with sharply contrasting chocolate and white markings on the sides of its face. The New Mexico Ridge-nosed Rattlesnake is grayish and lacks prominent facial markings. Pale cross bars ornament the backs of both forms. Young snakes have yellowish or black tails which they probably use to lure lizard prey. Adults have lightly striped tails, unlike most rattlesnakes which have banded or plain tails. Named for the small row of upturned scales on the snout. Predominantly adapted to woodlands, this snake is only found in Madrean Evergreen Woodland and Petran Montane Conifer Forest. Most abundant along heavily wooded canyon bottoms with adjacent open slopes. In Arizona, the New Mexico Ridge-nosed Rattlesnake is found only in the Peloncillo Mountains. The Arizona Ridge-nosed Rattlesnake is found in the Huachuca, Santa Rita, Patagonia, and Whetstone mountains, as well as the Canelo Hills. Adults feed mainly on small mammals, birds, and lizards, whereas juveniles feed primarily on lizards and giant centipedes. Weakly toxic venom. Mates July–September and gives birth to 2–9 young the next year, in July or August. The New Mexico Ridge-nosed Rattlesnake is listed as Threatened under the Endangered Species Act. The Arizona Ridge-nosed Rattlesnake is also protected.

Twin-spotted Rattlesnake
Crotalus pricei

Rock Rattlesnake
Crotalus lepidus

Arizona Ridge-nosed
Rattlesnake

Ridge-nosed Rattlesnake
Crotalus willardi

striped tail

New Mexico
Ridge-nosed Rattlesnake

adaptations: behavioral, physiological, or anatomical characteristics of organisms that confer fitness; traits that have or will spread through populations via natural or indirect selection

aestivation: a state of dormancy or low activity during hot dry seasons

alluvial: pertaining to clay, silt, sand, gravel, or similar material deposited by running water

amphisbaenians: elongate, annulated, and usually limbless reptiles belonging to the order Squamata

anterior: situated forward, toward the front end of a body

anuran: frogs, toads, and treefrogs from the order Anura

aquatic: living principally in water

arboreal: inhabiting trees and shrubs

Arizona Strip: the portion of Arizona north and west of the Colorado River

arroyo: a usually dry watercourse or creek bed in an arid region

arthropod: invertebrates of the phylum Arthropoda which include insects, arachnids, and crustaceans

axial: near or in the "armpit"

bajada: gently sloping, conjoined masses of alluvial gravel, sand, and earth that extend from mountain bases out into the surrounding valley

band: a marking that encircles the body or tail

bask: to lie in or expose oneself to warmth or sunshine

biodiversity: the number and frequency of different species of plants and animals in an environment

biome: an ecological community that has a distinct climate and assemblage of plants and animals

biotic community: a group of interdependent organisms inhabiting the same region and interacting with one another

bisected: divided into two equal parts

boss: a lump or projection

camouflaged: concealed or disguised, usually via crypsis

cannibals: species that eat their own kind

carapace: dorsal part of the shell of a turtle consisting typically of symmetrically placed bones overlaid by horny plates

carrion: dead and putrefied or dried animal flesh

chemoreception: physiological detection of chemical stimuli (*e.g.*, smell and taste in humans)

chevron: a shape consisting of two diagonal stripes meeting at an angle ▲

chin shield: large, flat, plate-like scale on the underside of the jaw

chytrid: an unusual group of aquatic fungi that are either decomposers or parasites of invertebrates; a new species, *Batrachochytrium dendrobatidis*, infects the skin of amphibians, is associated with amphibian declines, and is the first chytrid found to infect vertebrates

ciénega: a grassy wetland; a Spanish word literally translated as "100 waters"

cloaca: the common pouch into which the urinary, digestive, and reproductive organs discharge waste in birds, reptiles, amphibians, and many fishes

clone: an organism that is genetically identical to the organism that produced it

clutch: a nest or aggregate of eggs

concave: hollowed inward, like the inside of a bowl

constrictor: a animal that subdues its prey by squeezing it to death

cosmopolitan: distributed world wide

crepuscular: active around sunrise and sunset

cross-section: a section taken by cutting at a right angle to the main axis of a body

cryoprotectant: a substance that protects an organism from the effects of freezing

crypsis: a color, pattern, body shape, or behavior that results in an organism blending into its environment

cryptic: exhibiting markings and coloration that help to conceal

denizen: inhabitant, resident

disposition: an animal's prevailing temperament or behavioral tendencies

diurnal: active during the day

docile: calm, easily controlled

dorsal: pertaining to the back of an animal

dorsolateral folds: fleshy ridges of skin that run down both sides of back

ecological: related to the relationship of organisms and their environment

ecosystem: a dynamic and interrelating complex of plant and animal communities and their associated non-living environment

ecotone: a transition between two biotic communities

ectoparasite: a parasite that lives on the exterior of its host as opposed to within its body

Endangered (under Endangered Species Act): a species in danger of extinction throughout all or a significant portion of its range

endemic: restricted to a particular geographic area or biological community; an endemic organism

envenomation: injection of venom (which does not necessarily happen every time a venomous animal bites or strikes)

ephemeral: temporary, lasting only a short time

evert: to turn outward or "inside out"

excavate: to dig out and remove, as dirt from a burrow

external: on the outside

extirpated: completely removed from a defined area, locally extinct

exude: to ooze or pass gradually out of a body structure

forelimbs: the two limbs closest to the head of an animal

fossorial: adapted for digging and living underground

generalist: an animal whose habits or habitats are varied or unspecialized

genetically: relating to the transmission of qualities, encoded in the genes of an organism, from adults to offspring; ancestors to descendants

gills: respiratory organs used to obtain oxygen from water

glands: a cluster of cells that secrete liquid or viscous products, often organized in the form of prominent aggregations or as small organs

gracile: slender and graceful

gravid: full of eggs, pregnant

groin: the juncture of the lower abdomen and the inner part of the thigh

habitat: the set of environmental conditions under which a plant or animal naturally or normally lives, grows, and reproduces

hatchlings: recently hatched animals

hemorrhagic: causing internal bleeding

herbivorous: subsisting on plants for food

hibernaculum: a shelter used for hibernation

hybrid: an offspring of two different species

hybridizes: interbreeds and produces hybrids

ingest: to take in for food, swallow

internasals: the scales between the nasal scales, immediately posterior of the rostral

invertebrate: animal that lacks a spinal column

keeled: scales with a ridge ("keel") running down their length

larva: a form of an animal that at birth or hatching is unlike the parent and must metamorphose before assuming the adult form

larvae: plural of larva

lateral: relating to, or situated on, the sides

loreal: a scale found on the side of the head, between preocular and nasal scales (*see figure on page 94*)

lyre: harp-like instrument used by the ancient Greeks

marginal shields: the plates or shields around the outside edge of the carapace

mid-dorsal: in the middle of the back

monsoon: in Arizona, the summer season characterized by increased humidity and rainfall, often in the form of brief but intense thundershowers; usually lasting from early July through mid-September

mottling: blotchy or spotty markings

musk: a substance with a penetrating persistent odor excreted from the cloacal region

nasal valves: flaps in the nares that prevent debris from entering the nose when closed

neotenes: animals that attain adulthood (reproductive capability) in the larval form

neurotoxin: a substance that inhibits the function of neurons (nerve cells)

nocturnal: active at night

non-native: not naturally present in an area; introduced; exotic

omnivorous: eating both plants and animals

parietal: large plate-like scales on the top of the head (*see figure on page 94*)

parietal furrow: a (usually v-shaped) indention at the rear junction of the parietal scales (*see figure on page 94*)

parotoid glands: paired, puffy skin glands located on the rear aspect of the head of most bufonid toads and some hylid frogs that secrete chemicals that are toxic or irritating to potential predators

parthenogenetic: reproduces by development of an egg to form a zygote, without fusion of its nucleus with a male gamete; an asexual form of reproduction that results in all-female clonal lineages

pectoral girdle: in vertebrates, a bony or cartilaginous support structure to which the forelimbs are attached

perennial: present at all seasons of the year

petran: of or related to the Rocky Mountains

plastron: ventral part of the shell of a turtle consisting typically of symmetrically placed bones overlaid by horny plates

posterior: situated behind, the back end of the body

preanals: enlarged scales in front of the vent

pupae: an intermediate, immobile stage of a metamorphic insect (*e.g.*, bee, moth, or beetle) that occurs between the larval and adult forms

range: the geographic area occupied by populations of a species

raptors: a bird of prey (*e.g.* hawks, eagles, owls, and falcons)

refugia: a place of safety

reticulations: a net-like pattern consisting of two or more interlaced colors

riparian: an ecosystem that is transitional between land and water ecosystems, usually with terrestrial vegetation reflecting the influence of water

saddles: colored markings on the back of an animal that extend onto the sides, but do not encircle the body

scales: small, flat, rigid, and definitely circumscribed skin folds forming part of the external body

scute: a large scale

secrete: to release some sort of liquid substance

serrated: jagged-edged, like the teeth of a saw

solpugids: arachnids with large fangs and a segmented abdomen

spade: horny, dark projections on the hind feet of some toads that aid in burrowing backward into the soil

species: roughly, a "kind" of organism. More accurately, a population of organisms, distinguishable from other populations, in having shared individual characteristics and in terms of evolutionary relatedness

specimen: an individual

striations: parallel stripes or lines

stripe: a marking that runs lengthwise on the body

substrate: the surface on which, or in which, a plant or animal lives

supraoculars: the large scales above the eyes

taxa: classification groups, such as: family, genus, species

temperate: a moderate climate. not extreme or excessive

terminal: occurring at the tip or end of something

terrestrial: living principally on the ground or on land

thermoregulation: the maintenance of body temperature

Threatened (under Endangered Species Act): a species which is likely to become endangered within the foreseeable future throughout all or a significant portion of its range

toe pads: expanded areas on the tips of the digits of some frogs and geckos that aid in adhesion to vertical or upside down surfaces

topography: the characteristics of land surface including its appearance, texture, elevation, and relief

translucent: permitting the passage of diffuse light

trill: a pulsed musical sound

tubercle: a small knobby prominence or bump on an animal

tympanum: eardrum

vegetation: the plant growth forms that generally occupy a given area

venom: a toxic, glandular secretion that is actively delivered to the target organism, often injected by fangs or stingers, but sometimes delivered by chewing with grooved teeth

venomous: possessing glands for the secretion of venom

vent: the external opening of the cloaca

ventral: pertaining to the belly or underside of an animal

vertebral: paralleling the spine

vertebrate: animals that possess a spinal column (*e.g.* fish, amphibians, reptiles, birds, mammals)

xeric: characterized by dryness or low moisture

Glossary definitions adapted (in part) from:

Lees, Richard. Biology-Online.org. 2005. Online Biology Dictionary. http://www.biology-online.org/dictionary.asp Accessed 2005 February 23, 2006 January 2, and 2006 March 15.

Mirriam-Webster. 2005. Mirriam-Webster OnLine Dictionary. http://www.m-w.com/ Accessed 2005 February 23, 2006 January 2, and , 2006 March 15..

Photos taken by the authors are indicated by their initials.

Page vi: Arizona Upland Desertscrub, Butterfield Pass, Maricopa Mts., Maricopa Co., AZ (ATH). **Page 13:** Lower Colorado River Desertscrub, north of Mobile, Rainbow Valley, Maricopa Co., AZ (TCB); Arizona Upland Desertscrub, McDowell Mts., Maricopa Co., AZ (ATH). **Page 15:** Mohave Desertscrub, south of Meadview, Grapevine Mesa, Mohave Co., AZ (TCB); Chihuahuan Desertscrub, vicinity of Harris Mtn. north of Portal, Cochise Co., AZ (TCB). **Page 17:** Great Basin Desertscrub, Kanab Plateau, Coconino Co., AZ (TCB); Semidesert Grassland, vicinity of Oracle Junction, Pinal Co., AZ (David E. Brown). **Page 19:** Plains Grassland, vicinity of Lyman Lake, Apache Co., AZ (ATH); Interior Chaparral, Mazatzal Mts., Maricopa Co., AZ (ATH). **Page 21:** Madrean Evergreen Woodland, vicinity of Ruby, Pajarito Mts., Santa Cruz Co., AZ (TCB); Great Basin Conifer Woodland, Tonto Basin north of Rye, Gila Co., AZ (TCB). **Page 23:** Petran Montane Conifer Forest, Mount Ord, Mazatzal Mts., Maricopa Co., AZ (TCB); Subalpine Grassland, vicinity of Big Lake, White Mts., Apache Co., AZ (TCB). **Page 25:** Petran Subalpine Conifer Forest, Three Forks, White Mts., Apache Co., AZ (TCB); Alpine Tundra, Agassiz Peak, San Francisco Mtn., Coconino Co., AZ (TCB). **Page 29:** *Ambystoma tigrinum* (Barred Tiger Salamander), White Mts., Apache Co., AZ (Randy Babb); *Ambystoma tigrinum* (Sonoran Tiger Salamander), San Rafael Valley, Santa Cruz Co., AZ (TCB); *Ambystoma tigrinum* (Arizona Tiger Salamander), Mogollon Plateau, Coconino Co., AZ (TCB); *Ambystoma tigrinum* (aquatic larva), White Mts., Apache Co., AZ (Randy Babb). **Page 33:** *Scaphiopus couchii* (male), San Bernardino Valley, Cochise Co., AZ (TCB); *Scaphiopus couchii* (female), Maricopa Co., AZ (Erik Enderson); *Spea multiplicata*, vicinity of Holbrook, Navajo Co., AZ (TCB); *Spea bombifrons*, Sulphur Springs Valley, Cochise Co., AZ (TCB); *Spea intermontana*, Antelope Valley, Mohave Co., AZ (TCB). **Page 35:** *Bufo debilis*, Sulphur Springs Valley, Cochise Co., AZ (TCB); *Bufo retiformis*, Maricopa Co., AZ (TCB); *Bufo punctatus*, Pajarito Mts., Santa Cruz Co., AZ (TCB). **Page 37:** *Bufo microscaphus*, Mogollon Plateau, Coconino Co., AZ (Randy Babb); *Bufo woodhousii*, Roosevelt Lake, Gila Co., AZ (TCB); *Bufo cognatus*, Sulphur Springs Valley, Cochise Co., AZ (TCB); *Bufo alvarius*, Pajarito Mts., Santa Cruz Co., AZ (ATH). **Page 39:** *Gastrophryne olivacea*, Maricopa Co., AZ (TCB); *Craugastor augusti* (adult), Pajarito Mts., Santa Cruz Co., AZ (TCB); *Craugastor augusti* (juvenile), Eddy Co., NM (Charles W. Painter); *Smilisca fodiens* (adult), Maricopa Co., AZ (TCB); *Smilisca fodiens* (juvenile), Pima Co., AZ (TCB). **Page 41:** *Hyla arenicolor* (greenish), East Verde River, Gila Co., AZ (TCB); *Hyla arenicolor* (gray-brown), Pajarito Mts., Santa Cruz Co., AZ (ATH); *Hyla wrightorum* (green), Mogollon Plateau, Coconino Co., AZ (TCB); *Hyla wrightorum* (brown), Mogollon Plateau, Coconino Co., AZ (TCB); *Pseudacris regilla* (brown), Virgin Mts., Mohave Co., AZ (TCB); *Pseudacris regilla* (green), Virgin Mts., Mohave Co., AZ (TCB); *Pseudacris triseriata*, Mogollon Plateau, Coconino Co., AZ (Randy Babb). **Page 43:** *Rana berlandieri*, Salt River, Phoenix, Maricopa Co., AZ (TCB); *Rana blairi*, Sulphur Springs Valley, Cochise Co., AZ (TCB); *Rana pipiens* (green), Mogollon Plateau, Coconino Co., AZ (TCB); *Rana pipiens* (brown), Mogollon Plateau, Coconino Co., AZ (TCB). **Page 45:** *Rana onca*, Lake Mead, Clark Co., NV (TCB); *Rana yavapaiensis*, Sierra Ancha, Gila Co., AZ (TCB); *Rana chiricahuensis* (Mogollon Rim form), East Fork Black River, Apache Co., AZ (TCB); *Rana chiricahuensis* (southeastern Arizona form), Pajarito Mts., Santa Cruz Co., AZ (TCB). **Page 47:** *Rana tarahumarae*, southern Arizona, (TCB); *Rana catesbeiana*, Peña Blanca Lake, Pajarito Mts., Santa Cruz Co., AZ (TCB); *Xenopus laevis*, golf course pond in Tucson, Pima Co., AZ (Randy Babb). **Page 51:** *Terrapene ornata*, San Bernardino Valley, Cochise Co., AZ (TCB); *Chrysemys picta*, captive (TCB); *Trachemys scripta*, captive (TCB). **Page 53:** *Kinosternon arizonense*, Pima Co., AZ (Randy Babb); *Kinosternon flavescens*, San Simon Valley, Graham Co., AZ (TCB); *Kinosternon sonoriense*, Pajarito Mts., Santa Cruz Co., AZ (TCB). **Page 55:** *Chelydra serpentina*, Maricopa Co., AZ (Randy Babb); *Apalone spinifera*, Yuma Co., AZ (Jim Rorabaugh); *Gopherus agassizii*, Maricopa Co., AZ (TCB). **Page 59:** *Ctenosaura macrolopha*, captive (ATH); *Dipsosaurus dorsalis*, vicinity of Dateland, Yuma Co., AZ (TCB); *Sauromalus ater* (adult black back), Estrella Mts., Maricopa Co., AZ (TCB); *Sauromalus ater* (adult red back), Gila Bend Mts., Maricopa Co., AZ (TCB); *Sauromalus ater* (juvenile), South Mtn., Phoenix, Maricopa Co., AZ (TCB). **Page 61:** *Crotaphytus bicinctores*, Shivwitz Plateau, Mohave Co., AZ (TCB); *Crotaphytus collaris*, East Verde River, Gila Co., AZ (TCB); *Crotaphytus nebrius*, Yuma Co., AZ (William Wells); *Gambelia wislizenii*, Kanab Plateau, Mohave Co., AZ (TCB). **Page 63:** *Callisaurus draconoides* (dorsal), Yuma Desert, Yuma Co., AZ (TCB); *Callisaurus draconoides* (ventral), Maricopa Mts., Maricopa Co., AZ (TCB); *Cophosaurus texanus*, Upper Verde River, Yavapai Co., AZ (TCB). **Page 65:** *Holbrookia maculata*, Lukachukai, Apache Co., AZ (TCB); *Holbrookia elegans* (female), Pajarito Mts., Santa Cruz

Co., AZ (TCB); *Holbrookia elegans* (male), Santa Rita Mts., Santa Cruz Co., AZ (Bob Bezy). **Page 67:** *Uma rufopunctata* (dorsal), vicinity of Dateland, San Cristobal Valley, Yuma Co., AZ (TCB); *Uma rufopunctata* (ventral), Mohawk Dunes, Yuma Co., AZ (TCB); *Uma scoparia*, Cactus Plain, La Paz Co., AZ (TCB). **Page 69:** *Urosaurus graciosus*, Yuma Desert, Yuma Co., AZ (TCB); *Urosaurus ornatus*, West Fork Oak Creek, Coconino Co., AZ (TCB); *Uta stansburiana* (male), Gila Bend Mts., Maricopa Co., AZ (TCB); *Uta stansburiana* (female), Gila Bend Mts., Maricopa Co., AZ (TCB). **Page 71:** *Sceloporus slevini* (plain patterned), Huachuca Mts., Cochise Co., AZ (TCB); *Sceloporus slevini* (bold patterned), Huachuca Mts., Cochise Co., AZ (TCB); *Sceloporus virgatus*, Pinery Canyon, Chiricahua Mts., Cochise Co., AZ (TCB). **Page 73:** *Sceloporus graciosus*, Carrizo Mts., Apache Co., AZ (TCB); *Sceloporus tristichus* (blotched), Chinle Valley, Apache Co., AZ (TCB); *Sceloporus tristichus* (striped), Four Peaks, Maricopa Co., AZ (TCB); *Sceloporus tristichus* (throat), Four Peaks, Maricopa Co., AZ (TCB); *Sceloporus cowlesi*, (both full body and throat) Sulphur Springs Valley, Cochise Co., AZ (TCB). **Page 75:** *Sceloporus magister*, Superstition Mts., Pinal Co., AZ (Randy Babb); *Sceloporus clarkii*, Tonto Creek at Bear Flat, Gila Co., AZ (TCB); *Sceloporus jarrovii*, Garden Canyon, Huachuca Mts., Cochise Co., AZ (TCB). **Page 77:** *Phrynosoma cornutum*, Sulphur Springs Valley, Cochise Co., AZ (ATH); *Phrynosoma mcallii*, Yuma Desert, Yuma Co., AZ (TCB); *Phrynosoma platyrhinos*, Shivwitz Plateau, Mohave Co., AZ (TCB). **Page 79:** *Phrynosoma solare*, Cochise Co., AZ (ATH); *Phrynosoma hernandesi*, Mount Ord, Gila Co., AZ (TCB); *Phrynosoma modestum*, San Simon Valley, Cochise Co., AZ (TCB). **Page 81:** *Aspidoscelis exsanguis*, Cochise Co., AZ (Erik Enderson); *Aspidoscelis flagellicauda*, Tonto Creek at Bear Flat, Gila Co., AZ (TCB); *Aspidoscelis sonorae*, Florida Canyon, Santa Rita Mts., Pima Co., AZ (TCB); *Aspidoscelis neomexicana*, Petrified Forest National Park, Apache Co., AZ (Erik Enderson). **Page 83:** *Aspidoscelis uniparens*, Sulphur Springs Valley, Cochise Co., AZ (TCB); *Aspidoscelis velox*, Adamana, Apache Co., AZ (TCB); *Aspidoscelis arizonae*, Sulphur Springs Valley, Cochise Co., AZ (TCB); *Aspidoscelis pai*, Mazatzal Mts., Maricopa Co., AZ (TCB). **Page 85:** *Aspidoscelis xanthonota*, Sand Tank Mts., Maricopa Co., AZ (Erik Enderson); *Aspidoscelis burti* (small adult), Pajarito Mts., Santa Cruz Co., AZ (TCB); *Aspidoscelis burti* (large adult), Santa Catalina Mts., Pima Co., AZ (TCB); *Aspidoscelis tigris*, Dateland, Yuma Co., AZ (TCB). **Page 87:** *Eumeces callicephalus*, Pajarito Mts., Santa Cruz Co., AZ (TCB); *Eumeces multivirgatus* (adult), Anderson Mesa, Coconino Co., AZ (TCB); *Eumeces multivirgatus* (juvenile), Coconino Co., AZ (Erik Enderson); *Eumeces skiltonianus* (adult), Mohave Co., AZ (TCB); *Eumeces skiltonianus* (juvenile), Mohave Co., AZ (Erik Enderson). **Page 89:** *Eumeces gilberti* (adult), Bradshaw Mts., Yavapai Co., AZ (TCB); *Eumeces gilberti* (juvenile), Yavapai Co., AZ (Erik Enderson); *Eumeces obsoletus* (adult), San Bernardino Valley, Cochise Co., AZ (Randy Babb); *Eumeces obsoletus* (juvenile), Huachuca Mts., Cochise Co., AZ (Randy Babb); *Elgaria kingii* (adult), Pine Creek, Gila Co., AZ (TCB); *Elgaria kingii* (juvenile), Tonto Creek, Gila Co., AZ (TCB). **Page 91:** *Coleonyx variegatus*, Stanfield, Pinal Co., AZ (TCB); *Hemidactylus turcicus*, Phoenix, Maricopa Co., AZ (TCB); *Xantusia bezyi*, Mazatzal Mts., Maricopa Co., AZ (ATH); *Xantusia vigilis*, Harquahala Mts., Maricopa Co., AZ (TCB). **Page 93:** *Heloderma suspectum* (Reticulate Gila Monster), AZ (Randy Babb); *Heloderma suspectum* (Banded Gila Monster), ASU live collection (ATH). **Page 97:** *Leptotyphlops dissectus*, San Bernardino Valley, Cochise Co., AZ (TCB); *Leptotyphlops humilis*, Apache Junction, Maricopa Co., AZ (TCB); *Lichanura trivirgata* (Desert Rosy Boa), Harcuvar Mts., La Paz Co., AZ (TCB); *Lichanura trivirgata* (Mexican Rosy Boa), captive born, ASU live collection (ATH). **Page 99:** *Micruroides euryxanthus*, Pajarito Mts., Santa Cruz Co., AZ (TCB); *Chionactis palarostris*, Organ Pipe Cactus National Monument, Pima Co., AZ (TCB); *Chionactis occipitalis* (Colorado Desert Shovelnosed Snake), Yuma Desert, Yuma Co., AZ (Randy Babb); *Chionactis occipitalis* (Mohave Shovel-nosed Snake), Cactus Plain, La Paz Co., AZ (TCB); *Chionactis occipitalis* (Tucson Shovel-nosed Snake), vicinity of Florence, Pinal Co., AZ (TCB). **Page 101:** *Chilomeniscus stramineus*, Maricopa Co., AZ (ATH); *Sonora semiannulata* (plain), Maricopa Co., AZ (ATH); *Sonora semiannulata* (banded), Gila Bend Mts., Maricopa Co., AZ (TCB); *Sonora semiannulata* (striped), Maricopa Co., AZ (Randy Babb). **Page 103:** *Tantilla nigriceps*, Sulphur Springs Valley, Cochise Co., AZ (Randy Babb); *Tantilla nigriceps* (head detail), Sulphur Springs Valley, Cochise Co., AZ (ATH); *Tantilla hobartsmithi*, Maricopa Co., AZ (Jim Rorabaugh); *Tantilla hobartsmithi* (head detail), Maricopa Co., AZ (ATH); *Tantilla yaquia*, Pajarito Mts., Santa Cruz Co., AZ (ATH); *Tantilla yaquia* (head detail), Pajarito Mts., Santa Cruz Co., AZ (ATH); *Tantilla wilcoxi*, Huachuca Mts., Cochise Co., AZ (ATH); *Tantilla wilcoxi* (head detail), Huachuca Mts., Cochise Co., AZ (ATH). **Page 105:** *Diadophis punctatus*, Pajarito Mts., Santa Cruz Co., AZ (ATH); *Hypsiglena torquata*, vicinity of Florence, Pinal Co., AZ (TCB); *Trimorphodon biscutatus*, Gila Bend Mts.,

Maricopa Co., AZ (TCB). **Page 107:** *Pituophis catenifer*, Harquahala Mts., Maricopa Co., AZ (TCB); *Arizona elegans*, vicinity of Holbrook, Navajo Co., AZ (TCB); *Phyllorhynchus decurtatus*, Maricopa Co., AZ (ATH); *Phyllorhynchus browni*, Lake Pleasant, Maricopa Co., AZ (Randy Babb). **Page 109:** *Heterodon nasicus*, Sulphur Springs Valley, Cochise Co., AZ (ATH); *Gyalopion canum*, San Pedro Valley, Cochise Co., AZ (Jim Rorabaugh); *Gyalopion quadrangulare*, vicinity of Rio Rico, Santa Cruz Co., AZ (TCB). **Page 111:** *Oxybelis aeneus*, Pajarito Mts., Santa Cruz Co., AZ (ATH); *Salvadora grahamiae*, Pinaleño Mts., Graham Co., AZ (TCB); *Salvadora hexalepis*, Adams Mesa, Maricopa Co., AZ (TCB). **Page 113:** *Senticolis triaspis* (juvenile), Chiricahua Mts., Cochise Co., AZ (ATH); *Senticolis triaspis* (adult), Pajarito Mts., Santa Cruz Co., AZ (ATH); *Masticophis bilineatus*, Page Springs, Yavapai Co., AZ (TCB); *Masticophis taeniatus*, Cerbat Mts., Mohave Co., AZ (TCB). **Page 115:** *Masticophis flagellum* (black phase), vicinity of Florence, Pinal Co., AZ (ATH); *Masticophis flagellum* (red phase), Harquahala Mts., Maricopa Co., AZ (ATH); *Coluber constrictor* (adult), Torrance Co., NM (Marla Hibbits); *Coluber constrictor* (juvenile), Utah Co., UT (Louis Porras). **Page 117:** *Rhinocheilus lecontei* (black & white), Maricopa Co., AZ (ATH); *Rhinocheilus lecontei* (tri-color), vicinity of Florence, Pinal Co., AZ (TCB); *Lampropeltis getula* (California Kingsnake), captive, ASU live collection. (ATH); *Lampropeltis getula* (Western Black Kingsnake), captive, ASU live collection. (ATH); *Lampropeltis getula* (Desert Kingsnake), San Bernardino Valley, Cochise Co., AZ (ATH). **Page 119:** *Lampropeltis pyromelana*, Pajarito Mts., Santa Cruz Co., AZ (TCB); *Lampropeltis triangulum*, Coconino Co., AZ (TCB); *Lampropeltis triangulum*, San Bernardino Valley, Cochise Co., AZ (TCB). **Page 121:** *Thamnophis cyrtopsis*, Peloncillo Mts., Cochise Co., AZ (ATH); *Thamnophis elegans*, vicinity of Lyman Lake, Apache Co., AZ (ATH); *Thamnophis marcianus*, San Bernardino Valley, Cochise Co., AZ (TCB). **Page 123:** *Thamnophis eques*, Tonto Creek, Tonto Basin, Gila Co., AZ (TCB); *Thamnophis rufipunctatus*, Coconino Co., AZ (TCB). **Page 125:** *Crotalus atrox*, Maricopa Co., AZ (ATH); *Crotalus scutulatus*, Portal, Cochise Co., AZ (ATH); *Crotalus molossus*, Pajarito Mts., Santa Cruz Co., AZ (ATH). **Page 127:** *Crotalus cerastes*, Maricopa Mts., Maricopa Co., AZ (ATH); *Crotalus tigris*, South Mtn., Maricopa Co., AZ (ATH); *Crotalus mitchellii* (blue phase), Maricopa Co., AZ (ATH); *Crotalus mitchellii* (red phase), Phoenix Mts., Maricopa Co., AZ (TCB). **Page 129:** *Crotalus cerberus* (adult), Mazatzal Mts., Maricopa Co., AZ (TCB); *Crotalus cerberus* (juvenile), East Fork Black River, Apache Co., AZ (TCB); *Crotalus oreganus* (Great Basin Rattlesnake), Arizona Strip, Mohave Co., AZ (ATH); *Crotalus oreganus* (Grand Canyon Rattlesnake), Grand Canyon, Coconino Co., AZ (ATH); *Crotalus oreganus* (Midget Faded Rattlesnake), Utah (Randy Babb). **Page 131:** *Crotalus viridis* (Green Prairie Rattlesnake), vicinity of Eagar, Apache Co., AZ (Randy Babb); *Crotalus viridis* (Hopi Rattlesnake), Navajo Co., AZ (ATH); *Sistrurus catenatus*, San Bernardino Valley, Cochise Co., AZ (ATH). **Page 133:** *Crotalus pricei*, Chiricahua Mts., Cochise Co., AZ (ATH); *Crotalus lepidus*, Cochise Co., AZ (ATH); *Crotalus willardi* (Arizona Ridge-nosed Rattlesnake), Huachuca Mts., Cochise Co., AZ (ATH); *Crotalus willardi* (New Mexico Ridge-nosed Rattlesnake), Hidalgo Co., NM (ATH).

Salamanders

☐ *Ambystoma tigrinum* _____

Frogs & Toads

☐ *Bufo alvarius* _____
☐ *Bufo cognatus* _____
☐ *Bufo debilis* _____
☐ *Bufo microscaphus* _____
☐ *Bufo punctatus* _____
☐ *Bufo retiformis* _____
☐ *Bufo woodhousii* _____
☐ *Craugastor augusti* _____
☐ *Gastrophryne olivacea* _____
☐ *Hyla arenicolor* _____
☐ *Hyla wrightorum* _____
☐ *Pseudacris regilla* _____
☐ *Pseudacris triseriata* _____
☐ *Rana berlandieri* _____
☐ *Rana blairi* _____
☐ *Rana catesbeiana* _____
☐ *Rana chiricahuensis* _____
☐ *Rana onca* _____
☐ *Rana pipiens* _____
☐ *Rana tarahumarae* _____
☐ *Rana yavapaiensis* _____
☐ *Scaphiopus couchii* _____
☐ *Smilisca fodiens* _____
☐ *Spea bombifrons* _____
☐ *Spea intermontana* _____
☐ *Spea multiplicata* _____
☐ *Xenopus laevis* _____

Turtles

☐ *Apalone spinifera* _____
☐ *Chelydra serpentina* _____
☐ *Chrysemys picta* _____
☐ *Gopherus agassizii* _____
☐ *Kinosternon arizonense* _____
☐ *Kinosternon flavescens* _____
☐ *Kinosternon sonoriense* _____
☐ *Terrapene ornata* _____
☐ *Trachemys scripta* _____

Lizards

- ❏ *Aspidoscelis arizonae* _____
- ❏ *Aspidoscelis burti* _____
- ❏ *Aspidoscelis exsanguis* _____
- ❏ *Aspidoscelis flagellicauda* _____
- ❏ *Aspidoscelis neomexicana* _____
- ❏ *Aspidoscelis pai* _____
- ❏ *Aspidoscelis sonorae* _____
- ❏ *Aspidoscelis tigris* _____
- ❏ *Aspidoscelis uniparens* _____
- ❏ *Aspidoscelis velox* _____
- ❏ *Aspidoscelis xanthonota* _____
- ❏ *Callisaurus draconoides* _____
- ❏ *Coleonyx variegatus* _____
- ❏ *Cophosaurus texanus* _____
- ❏ *Crotaphytus bicinctores* _____
- ❏ *Crotaphytus collaris* _____
- ❏ *Crotaphytus nebrius* _____
- ❏ *Ctenosaura macrolopha* _____
- ❏ *Dipsosaurus dorsalis* _____
- ❏ *Elgaria kingii* _____
- ❏ *Eumeces callicephalus* _____
- ❏ *Eumeces gilberti* _____
- ❏ *Eumeces multivirgatus* _____
- ❏ *Eumeces obsoletus* _____
- ❏ *Eumeces skiltonianus* _____
- ❏ *Gambelia wislizenii* _____
- ❏ *Heloderma suspectum* _____
- ❏ *Hemidactylus turcicus* _____
- ❏ *Holbrookia elegans* _____
- ❏ *Holbrookia maculata* _____
- ❏ *Phrynosoma cornutum* _____
- ❏ *Phrynosoma hernandesi* _____
- ❏ *Phrynosoma mcallii* _____
- ❏ *Phrynosoma modestum* _____
- ❏ *Phrynosoma platyrhinos* _____
- ❏ *Phrynosoma solare* _____
- ❏ *Sauromalus ater* _____
- ❏ *Sceloporus clarkii* _____
- ❏ *Sceloporus cowlesi* _____
- ❏ *Sceloporus graciosus* _____

Lizards, continued

- ☐ *Sceloporus jarrovii* _____
- ☐ *Sceloporus magister* _____
- ☐ *Sceloporus slevini* _____
- ☐ *Sceloporus tristichus* _____
- ☐ *Sceloporus virgatus* _____
- ☐ *Uma rufopunctata* _____
- ☐ *Uma scoparia* _____
- ☐ *Urosaurus graciosus* _____
- ☐ *Urosaurus ornatus* _____
- ☐ *Uta stansburiana* _____
- ☐ *Xantusia bezyi* _____
- ☐ *Xantusia vigilis* _____

Snakes

- ☐ *Arizona elegans* _____
- ☐ *Chilomeniscus stramineus* _____
- ☐ *Chionactis occipitalis* _____
- ☐ *Chionactis palarostris* _____
- ☐ *Coluber constrictor* _____
- ☐ *Crotalus atrox* _____
- ☐ *Crotalus cerastes* _____
- ☐ *Crotalus cerberus* _____
- ☐ *Crotalus lepidus* _____
- ☐ *Crotalus mitchellii* _____
- ☐ *Crotalus molossus* _____
- ☐ *Crotalus oreganus* _____
- ☐ *Crotalus pricei* _____
- ☐ *Crotalus scutulatus* _____
- ☐ *Crotalus tigris* _____
- ☐ *Crotalus viridis* _____
- ☐ *Crotalus willardi* _____
- ☐ *Diadophis punctatus* _____
- ☐ *Gyalopion canum* _____
- ☐ *Gyalopion quadrangulare* _____
- ☐ *Heterodon nasicus* _____
- ☐ *Hypsiglena torquata* _____
- ☐ *Lampropeltis getula* _____
- ☐ *Lampropeltis pyromelana* _____
- ☐ *Lampropeltis triangulum* _____
- ☐ *Leptotyphlops dissectus* _____

Snakes, continued.

- ❏ *Leptotyphlops humilis* _____
- ❏ *Lichanura trivirgata* _____
- ❏ *Masticophis bilineatus* _____
- ❏ *Masticophis flagellum* _____
- ❏ *Masticophis taeniatus* _____
- ❏ *Micruroides euryxanthus* _____
- ❏ *Oxybelis aeneus* _____
- ❏ *Phyllorhynchus browni* _____
- ❏ *Phyllorhynchus decurtatus* _____
- ❏ *Pituophis catenifer* _____
- ❏ *Rhinocheilus lecontei* _____
- ❏ *Salvadora grahamiae* _____
- ❏ *Salvadora hexalepis* _____
- ❏ *Senticolis triaspis* _____
- ❏ *Sistrurus catenatus* _____
- ❏ *Sonora semiannulata* _____
- ❏ *Tantilla hobartsmithi* _____
- ❏ *Tantilla nigriceps* _____
- ❏ *Tantilla wilcoxi* _____
- ❏ *Tantilla yaquia* _____
- ❏ *Thamnophis cyrtopsis* _____
- ❏ *Thamnophis elegans* _____
- ❏ *Thamnophis eques* _____
- ❏ *Thamnophis marcianus* _____
- ❏ *Thamnophis rufipunctatus* _____
- ❏ *Trimorphodon biscutatus* _____